DEAD HEADS

Stage 6

How could roses be connected with murder? A rose garden in summer is a delightful place, full of colours and sweet scents and the peaceful hum of bees. It has nothing to do with jealousy, hate, greed, revenge – the usual motives for murder.

The gardens at Rosemont House are very beautiful, and Patrick Aldermann is justly proud of his roses. Indeed, he seems to think of little else, so it is all the more surprising when his boss, Dick Elgood, reports him to the police for attempted murder. 'Elgood's gone soft in the head,' says Chief Superintendent Dalziel, but, just in case, he tells Inspector Pascoe to investigate.

Pascoe would rather be catching burglars, but he begins dutifully to dig into Patrick Aldermann's past. Meanwhile, his wife, Ellie, becomes friendly with Aldermann's wife, and young Police Cadet Singh discovers some interesting information about visitors to Elgood's seaside cottage. Personal lives become mixed up with professional duties. However, Pascoe goes on digging, and begins to get excited, then more and more puzzled . . .

Reginald Hill (1936–) is a well-known writer of crime novels. His Dalziel and Pascoe detective stories are set in Yorkshire, where he himself lives.

OXFORD BOOKWORMS
Series Editor: Tricia Hedge

OXFORD BOOKWORMS

For a full list of titles in all the Oxford Bookworms series,
please refer to the *Oxford English* catalogue.

~ Black Series ~

Titles available include:

~ **Stage 1** (400 headwords)
*The Elephant Man *Tim Vicary*
*The Monkey's Paw *W.W.Jacobs*
Under the Moon *Rowena Akinyemi*
The Phantom of the Opera *Jennifer Bassett*

~ **Stage 2** (700 headwords)
*Sherlock Holmes Short Stories
  Sir Arthur Conan Doyle
*Voodoo Island *Michael Duckworth*
New Yorkers *O.Henry* (short stories)

~ **Stage 3** (1000 headwords)
*Skyjack! *Tim Vicary*
Love Story *Erich Segal*
Tooth and Claw *Saki* (short stories)
Wyatt's Hurricane *Desmond Bagley*

~ **Stage 4** (1400 headwords)
*The Hound of the Baskervilles
  Sir Arthur Conan Doyle
*Three Men in a Boat *Jerome K. Jerome*
The Big Sleep *Raymond Chandler*

~ **Stage 5** (1800 headwords)
*Ghost Stories *retold by Rosemary Border*
The Dead of Jericho *Colin Dexter*
Wuthering Heights *Emily Brontë*
I, Robot *Isaac Asimov* (short stories)

~ **Stage 6** (2500 headwords)
*Tess of the d'Urbervilles *Thomas Hardy*
Cry Freedom *John Briley*
Meteor *John Wyndham* (short stories)
Deadheads *Reginald Hill*

Many other titles available, both classic and modern.
**Cassettes available for these titles.*

~ Green Series ~

Adaptations of classic and modern stories for younger readers.
Titles available include:

~ **Stage 2** (700 headwords)
Robinson Crusoe *Daniel Defoe*
Alice's Adventures in Wonderland *Lewis Carroll*
Huckleberry Finn *Mark Twain*

~ **Stage 3** (1000 headwords)
The Prisoner of Zenda *Anthony Hope*
The Secret Garden *Frances Hodgson Burnett*
The Railway Children *Edith Nesbit*

~ **Stage 4** (1400 headwords)
Treasure Island *Robert Louis Stevenson*
Gulliver's Travels *Jonathan Swift*
A Tale of Two Cities *Charles Dickens*

OXFORD BOOKWORMS COLLECTION

Fiction by well-known authors, both classic and modern.
Texts are not abridged or simplified in any way. Titles available include:

From the Cradle to the Grave
  (short stories by *Saki, Evelyn Waugh, Roald Dahl,
  Susan Hill, Somerset Maugham, H. E. Bates,
  Frank Sargeson, Raymond Carver*)

Crime Never Pays
  (short stories by *Agatha Christie,
  Graham Greene, Ruth Rendell, Angela Noel,
  Dorothy L. Sayers, Margery Allingham,
  Sir Arthur Conan Doyle, Patricia Highsmith*)

DEADHEADS

Reginald Hill

retold by
Rosalie Kerr

OXFORD UNIVERSITY PRESS

Oxford University Press,
Walton Street, Oxford OX2 6DP

Oxford New York Toronto Madrid
Delhi Bombay Calcutta Madras Karachi
Kuala Lumpur Singapore Hong Kong Toyko
Nairobi Dar es Salaam Cape Town
Melbourne Auckland
and associated companies in
Berlin Ibadan

OXFORD and OXFORD ENGLISH
are trade marks of Oxford University Press

ISBN 0 19 422684 0

Original edition copyright © Reginald Hill 1983
First published 1983 by William Collins Sons & Co Ltd
This simplified edition © Oxford University Press 1993

First published 1993
Second impression 1993

Illustrated by Nick Hardcastle

Typeset by Pentacor PLC, High Wycombe, Bucks
Printed in England by Clays Ltd, St Ives plc

Part 1

Death in a rose garden

Mrs Florence Aldermann hated to see her garden looking so neglected. Her old gardener, Caldicott, and his son, Dick, had not been working properly. That was because she had refused to employ Dick's son Brent. Brent had stolen some fruit from her garden, and that was a serious crime to Mrs Aldermann. She would have to get rid of the Caldicotts.

With this thought in her mind, she took her sharp knife and angrily cut the dead flowers from a rosebush. As the deadheads fell into her bucket, she realized that someone was watching her.

'Patrick,' she called crossly, 'come here!'

Slowly the boy came up to her. Aged about eleven, he was still small for his age. His face was pale and expressionless.

Mrs Aldermann could never see Patrick without feeling angry. She had been angry when her niece Penelope had produced this unwanted child. She had been even angrier when Penelope refused to say who the father was. Mrs Aldermann's anger was strong and long-lasting. She still felt angry with poor Eddie Aldermann, her husband, for dying two years ago and leaving her alone to look after Rosemont, this big house and its demanding gardens. Finally, she was angry with herself for growing old and tired, angry with herself for having a heart attack while shopping in London six months ago.

1

It was lucky that Penelope had been with her when illness struck. Penny was sensible, calm, and an excellent nurse. Nothing upset Penny. She had shown no anger or bitterness, for example, when told that after Mr Aldermann's death the money he had given her for years would stop.

Florence Aldermann came out of her private hospital as soon as she was well enough to travel, and returned to Rosemont. Penny came with her and looked after her perfectly. The only problem was that where Penelope went, Patrick had to go too. Despite this, Mrs Aldermann had asked her niece to stay with her at Rosemont permanently. The house was too big for her to live in alone, and Penny would be grateful, she felt sure, to be offered a home in such a lovely part of Yorkshire. She could not believe her ears when Penelope said she was missing London, and would have to think about her aunt's offer. How could anyone prefer a tiny, dark London flat to a fine old house like Rosemont, with its beautiful gardens!

Mrs Aldermann was about to speak crossly to Patrick, but before she could open her mouth, the boy said, 'Uncle Eddie used to do that. Why do you do it?'

His interest surprised her. She spoke less angrily than she had planned to.

'When the flowers fade and begin to die,' she said, 'we have to cut them off, so that new flowers can grow. We call it deadheading.' As she spoke, she expertly sliced off another faded, sweet-smelling rose.

'Deadheading,' he repeated. 'So that the new young flowers can grow.'

'That's right, Patrick.'

She felt almost pleased with the boy. For the first time, she looked at him with interest. The Caldicotts had failed her, but what if Patrick could be trained to look after her roses? What an excellent – and cheap – gardener he might become!

She smiled at him.

'Here, Patrick, take the knife. I'll show you how to deadhead roses. Be careful. It's extremely sharp. It belonged to your great-uncle Eddie.'

Carefully, he took the knife in his hand.

'Let me see you remove this deadhead,' she ordered him. She took hold of a dead flower. 'Cut it just here, Patrick. Patrick! Are you listening to me?'

He looked from the knife to his great-aunt. His face was not quite so expressionless as usual. There was something new there. He ignored the dead rose, and slowly raised the knife so that the sunlight shone on the polished steel.

'Patrick!' said Mrs Aldermann, taking a step back.

The rose that she had been holding towards him escaped from her hand, and its thorns dug painfully into her arm. Then there were other, more violent sensations in her shoulder and neck, which had nothing to do with the rose thorns.

She screamed once before she fell backwards into the rose-bed. Petals from the dying roses rained down on her.

Patrick waited until all movement had stopped. Then he dropped the knife, and ran towards the house, shouting for his mother.

Part 2

CHAPTER 1

'I think someone is killing people'

Richard Elgood was sixty years old, but as he came towards Peter Pascoe, he moved like a dancer in his soft leather shoes.

Pascoe shook Elgood's hand and smiled.

'Sit down, Mr Elgood. How can I help you?'

Elgood did not smile, although he had a pleasant, cheerful face.

'I'm not sure how to begin, Inspector,' he said.

They both sat down. Pascoe waited, watching the man, noticing his silk tie, the gold tie-pin, the expensive cut of his suit.

'Please, Mr Elgood,' Pascoe said. 'Tell me about it.'

Elgood took a deep breath.

'There's this man. In our company. I think he's killing people.'

Pascoe was tired. He had been working for much of the previous night, waiting in a garden for some burglars who never came. He desperately wanted to sleep.

'Can you give me just a little more detail?' he asked.

'I certainly can,' Elgood said. 'I'd rather tell my friend Andy Dalziel, but if he trusts you, I'll trust you too.'

He smiled at Pascoe, and Pascoe said, 'Mr Dalziel's very sorry he can't see you himself.'

What Detective Chief Superintendent Dalziel had actually

said was, 'I haven't got time to waste on old Dick Elgood this morning. You look after him for me. And take him seriously. He's got a sharp mind, he's made more money than you or I will ever see, and he's got a lot of influence in this part of Yorkshire.'

'All right,' Pascoe had said, 'but who is Elgood? What does he do?'

'Oh, you've seen his name,' Dalziel had smiled, showing yellow teeth. 'We've all seen it many times.' Then he had gone, leaving Pascoe puzzled.

'Now, Mr Elgood,' Pascoe said. 'You say this man works for your company. What kind of company is it?'

'Ever use a toilet?' Elgood asked.

Pascoe stared at him, speechless.

'Then you've seen my name,' Elgood went on. 'We make toilets, sinks, all that kind of thing.'

'Of course!' Pascoe exclaimed. 'Elgood Ceramics. I should have known.'

'I built that company up with my own hands,' Elgood said proudly. 'I started with nothing, and got where I am through hard work and hard work alone.'

'And this . . . er . . . killer,' Pascoe said. 'He works for you, does he?'

'Yes.'

'Well, who is it? You must give me his name.'

Elgood hesitated. Then he said in a low voice, 'It's Aldermann. Patrick Aldermann.'

Later that day, Pascoe went to see Chief Superintendent Dalziel, and told him what Elgood had said.

Dalziel laughed. 'Dick's always been a bit odd, but I never thought he was actually soft in the head before!'

'Do you know him well?' Pascoe asked.

'Known him for years. He's quite a character, is old Dick. Did you notice the way he dresses, all silk shirts and gold rings? You wouldn't look twice at him in London, but you don't expect a plain Yorkshire boy to grow up into something like that. And the women! A new one every week, if you believe the gossip. Wish I had the secret of his success!'

'I see, sir,' Pascoe said. 'What exactly would you like me to do?'

'Tell me what you know so far.'

'Elgood thinks Aldermann has killed two men who worked for his company. Their names were Brian Bulmer and Timothy Eagles. Bulmer died in a car crash after the office party last Christmas. Eagles had a heart attack at his desk.'

'Why does Dick think Aldermann was involved?'

'I was about to tell you. Aldermann kept giving Bulmer drinks at the party, almost forcing him to drink too much to drive safely, Elgood says. And Aldermann shared an office with Eagles.'

'Why should Aldermann want to kill Bulmer and Eagles?'

'Aldermann is ambitious. Well, not exactly ambitious . . .'

'Make up your mind. Is he or isn't he?'

'Elgood doesn't think Aldermann is very interested in his job,' Pascoe explained, 'so he isn't really ambitious. But he needs more money. He would improve his chance of a better-paid job with Bulmer and Eagles out of the way.'

'Does Dick really believe that?' Dalziel said. 'Something else must have happened to make him come to the police. What was it?'

'You're right,' Pascoe said. 'Something did happen. It seems he had a quarrel with Aldermann last Friday. Elgood told Aldermann that he didn't intend to promote him, although Bulmer and Eagles had gone. Then he had to go out to a meeting, and after that he returned to his office and worked until late. When he turned on his desk lamp, he got a powerful electric shock. He thought it was just an accident. Then yesterday morning he went to open his garage door – one of those metal up-and-over doors. It came off its supports and almost crashed down on top of him. Fortunately, he just managed to jump out of the way. That's when he started to feel frightened.'

'Um,' said Dalziel. He scratched his huge stomach thoughtfully. 'Why doesn't Dick want to promote Aldermann?' he asked.

'Two reasons, sir. The first is simply that he doesn't think Aldermann is very good at his job. The second is office politics. There are some people on the company's Board of Directors who would like to weaken Elgood's position as Chairman, to take some of his power from him. They want Aldermann on the Board just because they know Elgood doesn't want him.'

'Is that a fact? I think we'd better have a look at Mr Aldermann for ourselves, don't you? Got any good ideas on how we can go and see him without making him suspicious?'

'Actually, I have, sir,' Pascoe said. 'Sergeant Wield has given me some interesting information about a car which was badly scratched, probably by vandals, while it was parked in town the other day. It seems the owner is a Mrs Daphne Aldermann, who lives at Rosemont House.'

CHAPTER 2

Daphne Aldermann makes a new friend

Patrick Aldermann was standing in the garden at Rosemont, breathing in the perfume of his roses. Golden, pink, yellow, and red, they were a beautiful sight, and he smiled to himself as he inspected the flowers he loved.

Life had been kind to Patrick. In his early thirties he still looked young and handsome. He was happily married, and had a son and a daughter, both at expensive private schools.

His moment of peaceful enjoyment in the garden did not last long. The sound of his daughter Diana's voice reminded him that today he had to drive her to school. Normally his wife Daphne did this, but her car had been damaged by vandals, and was at the garage, being repaired.

He also knew that before he left he must find time to speak to his gardeners. They were the Caldicotts, the same family who had worked for his great-aunt. The old man had died, and now Dick, his son Brent and two young assistants kept the gardens neat and tidy. One of them had left the greenhouse door open, and Patrick wanted to make it clear to all of them that this was a serious offence. In future it would be better if none of them entered the greenhouse at all.

Daphne Aldermann waited patiently for her husband, although she wanted to speak to her daughter's teacher that morning and was eager to go. She knew how important the garden was to Patrick. A tall, good-looking, blonde woman, she had married young, very soon after the terrible accident that had killed her father. Now, twelve years and two children later, she knew that she was very lucky – in every way but one. She did not feel she really knew her husband. He seemed to live in a different world from her, a world in which the future was as certain as the past. It was strange how frightening she found this.

The sun was shining as they left Rosemont, but by the time they reached Diana's school, the sky was black.

'Oh no!' Daphne said.

'Looks like rain, doesn't it?' Patrick said. 'Shall I wait and drive you into town?'

'No, thanks,' Daphne replied. 'I'm not afraid of a bit of rain. Look! That lot are here again.'

She pointed to a small group of women, who were standing near the school gate. Two of them had small children with them, and each was carrying a sign on which she had written her own message. PRIVATE SCHOOLS = PUBLIC DISASTER was one; another was FREE SCHOOLS FOR ALL CHILDREN.

'Don't speak to them,' Patrick advised her. 'Goodbye, dear.'

Fifteen minutes later, finding herself out in the street in a heavy shower, Daphne felt less happy about walking into town in the rain. She looked around for a friend, but all the other mothers had gone. As she hesitated on the pavement, she noticed a young woman with short black hair putting a baby into a rather old car. Daphne wondered if she had seen her before, and smiled hopefully.

'You look as if you need a lift,' the woman said.

'Thanks awfully. That's really most kind of you,' Daphne replied.

She opened the car door. As she did so, something on the back seat caught her eye. The words PUBLIC DISASTER seemed to jump out at her.

'It's all right,' the woman said. 'I won't talk about it.'

A cold wind was blowing rain onto Daphne's legs. She got in.

'What a lovely little boy!' she said brightly, looking at the baby, who was wearing blue clothes.

'Actually, she's a girl,' the woman said, 'and she isn't always lovely. The blue clothes are a test of people's automatic reactions. Why should pink mean a girl and blue a boy? Let me introduce my daughter, Rose.'

'And you,' Daphne said coolly. 'Are you Rose's mother or her father?'

For a moment the woman looked shocked. Then she threw back her head and laughed loudly.

'Mother,' she said. 'My name's Ellie. Ellie Pascoe. Rose and I are on our way to have a cup of coffee. Would you like to join us?'

'Why not?' Daphne said.

Ten minutes later Daphne found herself drinking milky coffee in the Market Café, where Ellie and Rose seemed to be well-known customers. It was cheerful and noisy and full of shopkeepers from the market. It was not the sort of place Daphne usually went to for coffee. She wondered if Ellie had brought her there deliberately, hoping to make her feel uncomfortable – a rich woman among the workers. She saw Ellie watching her in amusement, when suddenly all conversation in the café stopped. Looking up, Daphne saw that two policemen had come in. One was an elderly man, and the other a young Asian, hardly more than a boy.

The customers relaxed and started talking again as it became clear that the policemen only wanted a cup of tea. They were looking around for an empty table when, to Daphne's surprise, the older man came towards her and Ellie.

'Hello, Mrs Pascoe,' he said. 'How are you? How's little Rose?'

'We're fine, Mr Wedderburn. Who's your friend? I haven't seen him before.'

'This is Police Cadet Shaheed Singh,' Wedderburn said. 'I'm introducing him to the joys of traffic control. Singh, this is Mrs Pascoe, Detective Inspector Pascoe's wife.'

Ellie smiled at Singh.

'Will you join us?' she said.

The young man smiled back at her, but Wedderburn said, 'Thanks, but we can't. A quick cup of tea and then we must get back to work. Nice to see you, Mrs Pascoe.'

'Well,' Daphne said, when the men had gone, 'so I'm in with the police, am I?'

'My husband's in the police, yes,' Ellie replied, 'but I'm not. What does your husband do, Daphne?'

'He works for Elgood Ceramics.'

'So you take a big interest in sinks and toilets, do you?'

'Not really,' Daphne said, looking puzzled.

'Exactly,' Ellie said. 'We may be married, but we are still individual people, aren't we?'

'Yes, but it isn't as simple as that. What if I told you that my husband was involved in some crime? Wouldn't you feel you should tell your husband?'

Ellie thought about it for a moment. Then she said, 'I'm not sure. What if I told you my husband was investigating yours? Would you feel you had to tell him?'

Ellie smiled at Singh. 'Will you join us?' she said.

Before Daphne could answer, she was interrupted by a well-built, middle-aged lady, dressed in bright colours, who was coming towards them with a cup of coffee in one hand, and a large plate of chocolate cake in the other.

'Hello!' she cried. 'It's Daphne Aldermann, isn't it? Lovely to see you again! I always meant to keep in touch, but life gets so busy, doesn't it?'

She turned and waved at three men, who were sitting at a table on the other side of the café.

'Coming, darlings! Must rush, Daphne. Bye!'

'So you do know someone who comes here,' Ellie said. 'You should have asked your friend to sit down. She looks like an interesting character.'

'Do you really think so? Well, Mandy Burke is hardly one of my best friends. Her husband used to work with mine, until he died about four or five years ago. I've only met her once or twice since then. Anyway, I don't think Mandy would want to sit with two women and a baby when there are men she could be entertaining!'

Ellie laughed. She was finding this elegant lady a surprisingly amusing companion.

'Let me get you some more coffee, Daphne,' she said.

CHAPTER 3

The most important thing in life

Patrick Aldermann's office still had the name of Timothy Eagles on the door. That didn't upset him. As his colleagues knew, it was difficult to upset Patrick.

Elgood remembered the party they had had at the office the previous Christmas. He had noticed Aldermann talking to the financial director, Brian Bulmer, and he had also seen that Bulmer was drinking heavily. Dick Elgood, however, had his mind on other things. He was leaving the party early, to meet a lady. Hours later, the news reached him. Bulmer's car had crashed, minutes after the end of the party, and he was dead.

Dick Elgood had spent that Christmas alone at his holiday cottage by the sea. He thought a lot about Bulmer's death and about who should replace him on the Board of Directors. The best man would be the chief accountant, Timothy Eagles, who was good at his job and loyal to the company. Some of the directors, who were led by a man called Eric Quayle, wanted Patrick Aldermann, but Elgood would not listen to them.

Then Eagles had died, suffering a fatal heart attack as he sat at his desk. It soon became clear that Quayle and his group wanted to make a serious attack on Elgood's chairmanship. They supported Aldermann, not because he would make a good director, but because they knew Elgood didn't want him on the Board. During that year, Elgood found himself fighting a battle,

15

a battle for his survival as Chairman of the Board.

Aldermann himself appeared not to care whether he became a member of the Board or not. 'Honestly, Dick,' he had told Elgood last Friday, 'it doesn't bother me at all.'

This made Elgood so angry that he ended up shouting at Aldermann, 'If you ever get a place on the Board, it'll be over my dead body!' Patrick had continued to smile politely.

Yesterday Elgood had gone to the police with his story, but since then he had calmed down and regained his self-control. He knew that for him the most important thing in the world was to hold on to the power he had as Chairman of the Board of Directors.

He called his secretary into the room. 'I want you to check something for me,' he told her. 'Find out exactly when Mr Aldermann is taking his holiday this summer.' Then he rang a London number, and asked for Mr Raymond Easey.

In his office on the floor below, Patrick Aldermann was opening his private letters, one of which contained a thick bundle of papers. He, too, phoned someone in London, and then called his secretary in.

'I'll be away next Thursday and Friday,' he told her. He smiled in a way which made her think how young and handsome he still was. 'I think you can all manage without me for a couple of days,' he said.

When Aldermann got home that evening, he found Daphne's car back in the garage. It had been repaired, and he examined the new paint before he went into the house.

Diana ran to meet him. 'Mummy's outside,' she told him.

He lifted her onto his shoulders, and together they went to

find Daphne, who was relaxing in the garden. It had rained earlier, but now it was a perfect June evening.

'I see your car's back,' he said. 'Look! The rain's knocked some petals off the roses.'

'Leave them,' Daphne said. 'I'll get us a drink. Sit down and have a rest after your hard day at the office.'

She went into the house. In the distance, Patrick heard the front doorbell ring. A couple of minutes later Daphne came back, bringing the drinks, but also bringing two men with her. The older man was white, the younger Asian, but what made Patrick stare at them was the ugliness of the one and the beauty of the other.

'I'm Detective Sergeant Wield,' the ugly man said, 'and this is Police Cadet Singh.'

'How can I help you?' Patrick asked politely.

'Actually, darling, they want to see me,' Daphne said. 'It's about the car. We can talk in the house so that we don't disturb you.'

'You won't disturb me,' Patrick said. 'I'd be interested to hear what the police are doing, and to help if possible.'

'Very kind, sir,' Wield said. He wanted to have a good look at Patrick Aldermann, and to include him in the conversation if he could.

Wield turned to Daphne. 'Now, ma'am. On Monday this week you parked your car in the Station Street multi-storey car park. What time did you leave it?'

'Nine fifteen, I think. I took my daughter to school, and then drove into town to do some shopping.'

'And you didn't come back until after three o'clock. Did you spend the whole day shopping?'

'I'm afraid so,' Daphne laughed. 'When I got back, someone else had already found his car damaged, and the police were there.'

'And when you left your car, were there any others there?'

'I can't remember,' Daphne said. 'I might have been the first. Does it matter?'

No, Wield thought, it didn't matter. This plan of getting a good look at Aldermann was not going too well.

'Not many more questions,' he said. 'Do you know anyone who might want to harm you in some way?'

'By damaging my car?' Daphne said, surprised. 'But it wasn't just my car. Others were damaged, too.'

'I know. But the scratchings on your car might have been words. Words which suggest they knew it was a woman's car.'

'I'd left my hat in the car,' Daphne said. 'Anyone could see that.'

'What words were scratched on the car, Sergeant?' Patrick asked.

'Hard to say, sir,' Wield said uncomfortably. Dalziel would say those words, he thought. He'd enjoy embarrassing these people!

'Why would this person damage other cars, if these words were aimed only at my wife?'

'We have to try everything, sir,' Wield told him. 'For example, what about you? Do you have any enemies who might want to do you some harm? Anyone you know through your work?'

Patrick shook his head. 'I work for Elgood Ceramics. I can think of nobody there who dislikes me enough to do this.'

He was getting nowhere, Wield thought desperately. He

would have to tell Pascoe this visit was a waste of time.

Suddenly Diana, who had been looking shyly at Police Cadet Singh through her fingers, said, 'Mummy, can I show him my flowers?'

'Oh, I don't think . . .' Daphne began, but Singh jumped to his feet with a smile and said, 'Of course, I'd love to see them. Come and show me.'

'I hope you don't mind, sir,' Wield said to Patrick. 'He's a good lad. And your garden is a real treat to the eyes. Especially the roses.'

Patrick's smile was as happy as Singh's. 'It's a good year for them,' he said. 'Do you grow roses, Sergeant?'

'I'm afraid not,' Wield said. 'I've only got a very small garden.'

'There are roses for every garden.' Patrick's voice had changed, and was full of enthusiasm. 'Even the smallest garden has room for a few roses, if you choose the right varieties. And think of the excitement of planting a new variety, and watching the first roses open!'

'I see plenty of excitement in my job,' Wield laughed.

'Do you?' Patrick asked seriously. 'I find life holds surprisingly few surprises – outside my garden, I mean.'

'I really must see to the dinner,' Daphne said. 'And it's time Diana came in.' She spoke politely, but clearly she was eager for Wield and Singh to leave.

Patrick ignored this. 'Diana's perfectly happy,' he said. 'Just listen to her. And I must show the Sergeant one or two roses I'd like to recommend to him.'

He led Wield to a large greenhouse, where he picked up a bag and took a knife from a high shelf. The greenhouse was full of tools and there was a large wall-cupboard with a heavy lock on the door.

'Good to see you've got strong locks, sir,' Wield said approvingly.

'I have to be careful, Sergeant, with children about,' Patrick replied. 'I keep enough pesticide in that cupboard to poison an army.'

As they walked among the roses, he used the knife to cut off dying flowers, which he dropped into the bag.

'Surely you have help with the garden?' Wield said. 'You can't look after all this by yourself.'

'I have help,' Patrick told him, 'but I do as much as possible myself. This garden is the centre of my life. I dream of having more time to give to it. I think we are all damaged, don't you, by limits on the development of our true nature – limits forced on us by the hard necessities of life.'

Wield felt that the man was speaking directly to him, as if Patrick Aldermann could know his own unhappy story. Ugly as he was, Wield had loved, and had been loved. He was alone now, and he could not bear to think of his loneliness.

'That's a fine knife,' he said, wanting to change the way the conversation was going.

Patrick smiled. 'It belonged to my great-uncle. He created this garden. He loved it very much. Cutting off the dying flowers is a sad but necessary job for a gardener. A true lover of plants like my great-uncle always wants to do it quickly and kindly. He needs the sharpest knife possible.'

The sun flashed on the point of the knife.

'Now, let me show you these.'

His enthusiasm for his roses had something almost religious

about it. Wield found he envied the man, not for his house, his garden or his family, but just because he knew so well what he wanted from life, and was able to enjoy it. He felt sad when Daphne called Patrick to dinner, and it was time for them to go.

'I hope it was all right for me to play with the little girl,' Singh said to him as they walked to the car. 'I thought it would give you more time to speak to her mum.'

Wield stared at him for a moment, forgetting that Singh knew nothing about the real reason for their visit.

'That Mrs Aldermann,' the boy went on, 'she was in the Market Café this morning, and guess who she was with? Mr Pascoe's wife!'

Wield stared at him again, coldly this time. 'You were supposed to be on traffic duty, not hanging around the Market Café,' he said roughly. They drove back to the Police Station in silence.

CHAPTER 4

Another death at Elgood Ceramics

Peter Pascoe was dancing baby Rose on his knee. 'Silly old Dalziel, silly old Dalziel,' he sang to her over and over again.

'What's the fat creature done to you now?' Ellie asked, as she came into the room.

'Fat creature! What a way to talk about your daughter,' Pascoe said.

'Very funny. What has Dalziel done?'

'Oh, nothing much. He just goes on about this Elgood and Aldermann thing. But I don't know what he wants me to do. Wield went to see them last night . . .'

'The Aldermanns?'

'Yes. He pretended it was all about your friend Daphne's car.'

'What did he find out?'

'Nothing.'

Pascoe did not plan to discuss with his wife all the poisons that Patrick Aldermann kept in his greenhouse. There was no proof that he had used them on anything but insects. There was no proof that Elgood's experiences with the desk lamp and the garage door were anything but accidents.

'I'll have to tell Elgood he's imagining things,' Pascoe said. 'He's been lying in the sun too long at his holiday cottage.'

'All the same,' Ellie said, 'Elgood Ceramics doesn't seem a

very healthy place to work. All those sudden deaths. This child is wet, by the way.'

'Only two deaths we know about. It's your turn to change Rose. I'm waiting for a phone call from the office.'

'Don't let Andy Dalziel work you so hard!'

'He's a good policeman,' Pascoe said seriously. 'He knows what he's doing, or I hope he does! Anyway, he's going to a conference in London, and I expect this stupid business about Aldermann will be over by the time he gets back.'

'Well,' said Ellie, 'if it does continue, I hope you'll tell me. It makes it rather awkward for me if my husband is investigating my new friend's husband.'

She picked Rose up and took her upstairs. As she went out of the room, the telephone rang. Pascoe picked it up, spoke a few words, and then listened carefully.

'I asked them to check for me,' he told Ellie when she came back downstairs. 'There has been one more death at Elgood Ceramics. A man called Burke fell off a ladder outside his home. Accidental death, the report said. No suspicious circumstances. He was assistant to Eagles, the chief accountant.'

'And Aldermann got *that* job?'

'Yes. It doesn't mean anything, of course, but I'll ask Elgood about it. By the way, when are you seeing Daphne Aldermann again?'

'We're having coffee tomorrow. Why?'

'Nothing. What's she like?'

'Pleasant. Lively. Very traditional middle-class attitudes, of course, but she's not stupid.'

'Attractive?'

'Oh, yes. Attractive all right. Rather sexy, really.'

CHAPTER 5

'Forget I ever came to see you'

Next afternoon Pascoe went to see Elgood in his office. He found him eating a sandwich at his desk, looking rushed and nervous.

'Had your lunch?' Elgood asked him. 'Lucky man! Can't talk to you for long. Got a meeting to go to.'

'These are tough times in business,' Pascoe said.

'Yes. Look, I'm beginning to feel I've been a bit soft, coming to see you. I should have thought about it first. Last thing I want is policemen all over the office, asking people questions. I got a bit upset the other day, that's all.'

Pascoe said nothing. Then he put a bag down on Elgood's desk. 'Your lamp,' he said. 'We've checked it. And the garage door. There's no proof there was any criminal action. No proof there wasn't, either.'

'I see. Looks as if I've made a bit of a fool of myself, doesn't it? Thanks for calling, Inspector.'

'One more thing. A man called Burke used to work here, didn't he?'

'Yes. What about it?'

'He fell off a ladder and broke his neck, didn't he? And then Patrick Aldermann got his job. Looks a bit suspicious.'

'Doesn't mean a thing,' Elgood said. 'An accident. And anyway, it was four years ago! Well, I'm a busy man, and I

Pascoe found Elgood eating a sandwich at his desk.

suppose you are too. At least I've given Andy Dalziel something to laugh about.'

Pascoe was about to leave the office, when he caught sight of a photograph on the wall. Elgood was in the centre of it, a confident smile on his face. Among the names underneath the photo was Aldermann.

'Who's that?' Pascoe asked. 'Any relation to our Patrick?'

'His great-uncle,' Elgood said. 'Eddie Aldermann. A great man, was Eddie. Very good accountant. Could have been very rich, but he spent it all on that big house, Rosemont. His wife, Florence, wanted the big house, and Eddie wanted the garden, and that's where the money went.'

'Any children?'

'No.'

'So they left the house to Patrick?'

'No. It went to Flo Aldermann's niece, Penny Highsmith. Nice girl, was Penny. Patrick's her son.'

'So she's Penny Highsmith and he's Patrick Aldermann. How is that?'

'Oh, Patrick thought the sun shone out of Eddie,' Elgood said. 'Changed his name to Aldermann, didn't he? Wanted to be a second Eddie. Well, he can grow roses all right, but he's not the accountant Eddie was, not by a long way.'

'Yet you gave him a job?'

'Why not? For Eddie's sake. Patrick was working for a company in Harrogate for a bit, but then he left. He didn't find a new job too easily. I think myself he was living on his great-uncle's money, spending most of his time on those gardens of his. The job with us was only temporary, but then Chris Burke died, so Patrick took his place.'

'But he isn't a great success?'

'He doesn't do too badly,' Elgood said. 'His heart isn't in it, though. He isn't really interested. People like him. He has charm, has Patrick. Look, I must go now. Forget I ever came to see you. Forget what I said about Patrick Aldermann. You understand me, don't you? Just drop it!'

Pascoe was left alone. As he walked out of the building, a tall dark man went through the door just ahead of him. He stopped to get into a car, and Pascoe noticed the beautifully shaped rose he wore in his buttonhole. It was a most unusual pinky-blue colour. Surely, this had to be Patrick Aldermann.

As Pascoe passed the car, he exchanged greetings with the man, who then said, 'Can I give you a lift?'

'No, thanks,' Pascoe replied, 'I've got my own car here. Excuse me, but I can't help looking at your rose. What a fascinating colour!'

'Do you like it?' the man said. 'It's called *Blue Moon*. Please take it.'

'Oh, I couldn't!'

'Why not? Blue Moon means improbability. We all need a little improbability in life, don't we? We must find the courage to reach out and take what life offers us.'

He put the rose in Pascoe's hand.

CHAPTER 6

Shaheed Singh investigates

Police Cadet Shaheed Singh was in a difficult situation. Walking past the shops on his way to the Police Station, he had met a couple of his old schoolfriends. They seemed pleased to see him and, as they had no jobs, they had plenty of time to ask him about his, and to admire his uniform.

The trouble was, the group had grown bigger, some silly games had started, and now they had taken his hat, and everyone was trying it on and laughing. He wanted to be friendly, but he also wanted his hat back, and he didn't know how to get it.

'Excuse me, Officer,' a woman's clear voice cut through the laughter. 'Can you help me, please? I'm looking for the Chantry Coffee House. Can you direct me to it? Are you going that way yourself?'

'Yes, of course,' Singh said. He held out his hand, and someone gave him his hat. He put it on carefully.

When they had walked a short distance, he said, 'Thank you, Mrs Pascoe. They're not bad lads, you know. They just haven't got anything else to do.'

'You're luckier than they are,' Ellie said. 'You found a job.'

'Oh, I could have worked in my dad's shop,' Singh said. 'I thought I'd rather be in the police.'

'And are you enjoying it?'

'It gets a bit boring sometimes. I'm ambitious, Mrs Pascoe. I want to do really well and get promoted fast.'

He stopped as they reached the Coffee House, and he could see Mrs Aldermann waiting for her inside. It did not surprise him that she and Mrs Pascoe were friends. To him the two women seemed very similar – confident, middle-class women who never had to worry about things like money. This thought would probably have annoyed Ellie, who considered that she was much more modern and progressive than Daphne.

Police Cadet Singh walked back to the station, thinking about Mrs Aldermann. He could not understand why Sergeant Wield had wanted to talk to her for so long about her car. He had no idea that Wield was interested in Patrick Aldermann.

When he arrived at the station, the first person he saw was David Bradley, one of the men who had been sent to the car park to examine the damaged cars.

'Got a moment?' Singh asked him.

'What's up, young Shady?' Bradley asked.

'That Mrs Aldermann. The one whose car was damaged. Wield's been asking her questions.'

'Wield? Why's he interested? There's nothing to say about her. A man called us. He was angry because his car had been scratched. She didn't seem to care. Just wanted to jump in the car and go, without speaking to us.'

'Didn't she have to stop and put all her shopping in the back of the car?'

'Shopping? She didn't have any. What's all this about, young Shady? Are you after Mr Dalziel's job already?'

'Just trying to learn how it's done,' Singh said. 'Did you say all the cars had been parked there by nine?'

'Yes. All right, Sherlock Holmes? Is that enough for you?'

'Thanks,' Singh said. He wished Bradley wouldn't talk to him as if he were an annoying child. Nobody else was treated like that. Did they do it to him just because he was black? He would show Bradley! He would show them all just how good at his job he could be!

'If Elgood says forget it, then forget it,' Dalziel said.

'I'm sorry, sir,' Pascoe told him, 'but I feel there's something wrong. What's strangest of all is that Elgood told us Aldermann had killed Bulmer and Eagles, but he's sure Burke's death was an accident.'

'Dick will have a reason, believe me,' Dalziel said. 'Remember, he's no fool. He's playing some game. We'll find out sooner or later what it is.'

'Well, I didn't have much luck,' Pascoe went on, 'but I did meet Aldermann. He gave me a blue rose.'

'He showed me his roses, too,' said Wield, coming in quietly. 'He was difficult to talk to at first, but he really came to life when he talked about the roses.'

'More interested in the roses than in his family?' Pascoe asked.

'Plenty of men are more interested in their hobbies than their families,' Dalziel said sharply. 'It's not a crime yet.'

'He really loves those roses,' Wield said. 'You should see him deadheading them, sir. He's got a special sharp knife. He uses it so skilfully.'

'I hope you're not suggesting that just because he cuts the heads off roses with his nice shiny knife, he does the same to people!'

'No, of course not, sir,' agreed Wield.

'So why should we waste time on this business?'

'Curiosity, sir,' Pascoe said immediately.

'Curiosity?'

'Yes. I want to know how this man, who isn't very good at his job, has got so far. He may be about to join the Board of Directors of an important company.'

'Half the people in top jobs don't deserve them,' Dalziel said. 'Listen, he sounds like Mr Average to me. Dull, ordinary; wife and two children, nice house, nice garden. I expect he even has a dear old mother.'

'I can tell you about that lady,' Pascoe said. 'Mrs Penelope Highsmith. Lives in London.'

'Highsmith? Why not Aldermann? Did she marry again?'

'She's never been married. Patrick chose to take his great-uncle's name. She's never told anyone who Patrick's father was.'

Dalziel didn't seem to be listening. Suddenly he burst out, 'Penny Highsmith! Did she live here?'

'Yes. Patrick went to school here.'

'I know her! I remember her well. She was a grand girl, full of fun. It must be her!'

The look in his eye told Pascoe that he had happy memories of Penny Highsmith. A smile lit up his fat face.

'I'll tell you what,' Dalziel said. 'I've got to go to this bloody conference in London. I'll be away a couple of days. You can see what you can do with this business while I'm away. Don't waste time on it, though. Now go away. I've got things to do.'

CHAPTER 7

How Daphne's father died

Daphne Aldermann was amused to find that Ellie and Rose visited the Chantry Coffee House as often as the Market Café.

'The coffee's better here,' Ellie said.

'But I'm sure you disapprove of the people, don't you?' Daphne said, looking round at all the middle-aged, middle-class ladies.

'I'm not sure I like crowds of any kind of people,' Ellie said. 'One at a time they're different.'

'When you're in the church, as my father was,' Daphne said, 'you have to accept all kinds of people. And they usually bang on your door asking for help just at dinner time!'

'Your poor father,' Ellie said. 'Or do you feel sorry for your mother, who had cooked the dinner, and then had to see it go cold?'

Daphne smiled. 'I suppose you want to suggest my mother had a miserable life in a male-centred family. In fact, I did the cooking. Mummy died when I was just a child.'

'Well,' Ellie said, 'people shouldn't have to ask the church for help. The state should provide for their needs.'

Daphne laughed. 'Come on! You don't know a lot about human nature, do you? Everyone knew Daddy was a kind man, and he had plenty of money. Mummy came from a rich family, you see.'

She looked sad, so Ellie said cheerfully, 'At least that meant he could afford some help in the house after you got married.'

'No.' Daphne looked close to tears. 'He was dead by that time. It was awful. He had to go to Little Leven to inspect the church, because the tower needed repairing. A stone fell on him and killed him.'

'I'm so sorry,' Ellie said gently. 'What a terrible thing to happen.'

She wondered whether to put an arm around Daphne, but was uncertain what to do. Fortunately, at that moment Rose plunged her hand into a chocolate cake, and Daphne's sad story was forgotten in the confusion. They talked for another hour before arranging to meet again the following week.

Ellie and Peter Pascoe had a late dinner that night. He had been delayed by another burglary at a local country house, while she had a crying baby to keep her busy.

Over dinner she told him about Rose's adventure with the chocolate cake, and went on to talk about Daphne.

'She was only seventeen when she met Patrick. He was an accountant in Harrogate, and did some work for her father's church. When they decided to get married, her father wasn't happy about it. Thought she was too young. Then he died. I think she still feels guilty for upsetting him just before his death.'

'How did he die?'

'The church killed him,' Ellie said mysteriously.

'Overwork?'

'No. A stone from Little Leven church tower fell on him.'

Pascoe whistled. 'People seem to drop dead right and left

34

around Patrick Aldermann, don't they?' he said. 'Interesting information! You're doing well!'

'Now look!' Ellie said. 'Daphne's my friend. I was just having a nice gossip, not acting as a police informer. I thought you told me all the business about Patrick murdering people was just nonsense.'

'I think it is,' Pascoe said. 'But do you mean you wouldn't tell me if you knew something that suggested he *was* a murderer?'

A sudden cry from Rose put an end to their discussion of this interesting but puzzling question.

CHAPTER 8

Daphne's secret

Shaheed Singh was at the top of the multi-storey car park where Daphne Aldermann's car had been damaged.

Ever since his visit to Rosemont with Sergeant Wield, he had been thinking about the case. He wanted so badly to do something right, to be a success as a policeman. Most of his old schoolfriends had no jobs. He supposed he was lucky, but at the moment he didn't feel it. Important men like Dalziel and Pascoe never noticed him, Sergeant Wield seemed to think he was a fool, and some of the others – well, he was sure they disliked him just because he was black.

He looked at his watch. Time to go. Wedderburn would be waiting for him for more boring traffic control.

At that moment the lift doors opened and five youths got out. He knew two of them, Jonty Marsh and Mick Feaver. They had been in his class at school.

'Hello, Shady!' they yelled. 'What's going on?'

'Someone's been damaging cars,' he told them, thinking quickly. 'We've got to catch them.'

'We!' laughed Jonty. 'There's only you here. *You'll* never catch anyone!'

'No,' Singh said seriously. 'You don't understand. The others are hidden, waiting. I've been sent out to have a word with you, because I said I knew you at school.'

He wasn't sure if Jonty believed him, but Mick and the others looked frightened and guilty. Singh had suspected his old friends. Now he was becoming sure that they had done the damage. He went on, half proud of himself, half ashamed of his power over these boys.

'The thing is, there's more to this than damage to a few cars. There's one car we're very interested in. If you have any information about it, you'll be helping us, and we always try to be nice to people who do that.'

He described Daphne's car to them. What happened next was better than anything he could have expected.

'Yeah, we saw her all right!'

'Blonde hair, yeah, tasty piece she was!'

'We know what she was getting into his car for!'

In a few minutes Shaheed Singh discovered that Daphne Aldermann had parked her car and got straight into another one. It was a big car, a BMW, and there was a man at the wheel.

CHAPTER 9

Is Patrick Aldermann a thief?

Peter Pascoe also found he couldn't stop thinking about the Aldermann case. It was nonsense, he was sure, but it fascinated him. Elgood must be suffering from overwork, and his imagination was working overtime. Pascoe knew all about stress, and the peculiar things it did to the mind. He had no time to spare for this nonsense, he told himself, as he picked up the phone and asked for Detective Inspector Skelwith of Harrogate police. He asked him to find out if they had any information about Patrick Aldermann, who used to work as an accountant in Harrogate.

'I'll try,' Skelwith promised. 'I wanted to talk to you, anyway. It looks as if the burglars you've had in your area have been at work over here.'

'Does it?' Pascoe said. 'Why don't I come over and see you this afternoon?'

He spent an hour at the burgled house with Skelwith, comparing the methods used with his own burglaries, and later, over tea at the office, came the reward Pascoe had hoped for.

'Aldermann worked for Bailey and Capstick,' Skelwith told him. 'He lost his job, it seems, and he was lucky it ended there. My advice, if you want the whole story, is to go and see old Capstick. He's retired, now. His address is Church House, Little Leven.'

*

Herbert Capstick seemed pleased to meet Pascoe. The old man lay in a wheelchair, looking out of the window at his pretty garden, beyond which Pascoe could see a church. This must be the church where Daphne's father had been killed.

Tea was served by a housekeeper, and Pascoe explained carefully that his enquiries were not really official; he only wanted to satisfy his own curiosity.

'Any information you give me,' he said to the old man, 'will of course remain confidential.'

Herbert Capstick looked at him thoughtfully for a moment, and then smiled. 'Very well, Mr Pascoe. I will tell you about Patrick. He came here as a young, newly qualified accountant. He was quiet, not particularly good at his job, but pleasant enough. I knew his great-uncle Edward very well. He was a very successful accountant. He made enough money to buy that old house, Rosemont, and rebuild that wonderful garden. Patrick loved Eddie, loved to talk about him, although he had only met him a few times. You know he changed his name from Highsmith to Aldermann? He had Eddie's love of roses, too.'

The old man pointed out into the garden.

'Look at those roses. Eddie planted some for me, more than thirty years ago. I've got just one of those left now. Patrick replaced the rest for me when they got too old. Roses grow old, Mr Pascoe, just like people. Patrick said the old must give way to the new, but the new must deserve their place. Look at them. Aren't they beautiful?'

They were, Pascoe could see, lovely roses, but he was eager for Capstick to get on with his story.

'Why did Patrick leave Bailey and Capstick?' he asked.

The old man looked sad.

This must be the church where Daphne's father had been killed.

'He was dishonest. Quite unexpected. A terrible shock to me. You see, there was an old lady, Mrs McNeil. She had a lot of money, and she wanted Patrick to manage it for her. He's very charming, you see, and she trusted him. She thought he was wonderful. Then one day he was not in the office when she called. There was a lot of flu around at the time, and he had caught it. Mrs McNeil wanted something, and I had to look at the books. Then I discovered what he had been doing. For three or four years, Mr Pascoe, he had been carefully and steadily stealing her money.'

He paused, and shook his old head sorrowfully. 'I had to tell him what I had found. He didn't deny it, just listened to me quietly.'

'Didn't you go to the police?'

'First I had to tell Mrs McNeil,' Capstick said. 'With her lawyer present, of course. But I had no opportunity. Patrick was soon well again, but Mrs McNeil had also got the flu. She was an old lady, and it was enough to kill her. So she died, you see, before I could tell her.'

Pascoe kept his face expressionless. 'But what about her will, and the relations who would have inherited?'

'She had left her money to Patrick Aldermann,' Capstick said. 'The only person he had cheated was himself. In the end, I decided, there was no point in going to the police. I told him to leave, and I said I intended never to see him again. I miss him sometimes,' he added sadly. 'I should like to talk about roses with him again.'

As Pascoe got up to leave, he said, 'That must be the church where the Reverend Somerton was killed. Daphne Aldermann's father.'

'Yes,' Capstick said. 'Oliver Somerton was a good man. A

42

little too serious in his ways, but a very good man.'

'You knew him? Of course, your company took care of his church accounts.'

'Yes,' Capstick said, 'but not just the church accounts. We looked after his own money, too. He was quite a rich man, as I expect you know.'

As Pascoe drove away, he could not help imagining the scene. Patrick Aldermann meeting the pretty young daughter, and then later finding some excuse to look at the account books to see how much money her father had.

Back at the station, he was surprised to find Sergeant Wield waiting for him with Shaheed Singh.

'Police Cadet Singh has something interesting to tell you, sir,' Wield said.

CHAPTER 10

Dalziel meets Penny Highsmith

Andrew Dalziel was bored. He didn't much like conferences. It was all right meeting old friends and having a few drinks with them, but apart from that he hadn't found much to interest him.

On his second afternoon in London he took a street map and set out to find Penelope Highsmith's flat. He found the house, and wandered around for a while, keeping an eye on the front door. He was lucky. He was just passing the building for the third time when a taxi stopped just outside and a woman got out. He recognized her at once. Tall and well-dressed, with thick black curly hair, she looked much younger than he had expected. He stopped, as if in sudden surprise.

'Penny?' he called. 'Is it really you, Penny Highsmith?'

'Yes,' the woman said. 'Who the hell are you?'

'Andy Dalziel,' he said. 'Do you remember me?'

'Of course. Weren't you in the police? You've put on weight.'

'Just a bit,' Dalziel said, smiling. 'I'm down here for a conference.'

'Still a policeman?'

'Yes.'

'Still married?'

'No.'

He waited.

'Coming in for a cup of tea, then?' she said.

Once inside her comfortable flat, he relaxed in a deep armchair and watched her as she moved around, making the tea.

She was much as he'd known her years before; warm, independent, cheerful – and very attractive. It's not fair, he thought. I've got old and fat, and she hasn't.

'Why did you leave Yorkshire?' he asked.

'I always intended to come back to London,' she told him. 'I only went to Yorkshire to look after Aunt Florence for a short while. Then she died, and I got the house and the money. By that time my son was at school. He loved Yorkshire.'

'Is he still there?'

'Oh yes. Still at Rosemont. He married a nice girl. They've got two children. I go up and visit sometimes, just for a day or two. I prefer my little flat here to that great big house.'

'I'm surprised you didn't sell it.'

'I nearly did,' she said. 'Patrick was just about to finish school and start work. It would have been a good time to make a move.'

'What happened to stop you?'

'The buyer died,' Penny Highsmith said.

CHAPTER 11

Who was Daphne meeting?

'You must tell us their names,' Wield said.

Shaheed Singh felt trapped, ashamed of being disloyal to his old friends, yet desperate to succeed in his job.

'Why?' he asked. 'I thought you were just interested in that Mrs Aldermann.'

'Let us decide who or what we're interested in,' Wield thundered. 'Your job is to obey orders!'

Why does he hate me so much? Singh thought miserably.

In fact, Wield felt sorry for the boy. But Pascoe had spoken to Dalziel on the telephone, and Dalziel had decided the boy must be questioned.

'You've got to tell us,' Wield said more gently. 'Maybe it won't be so serious for them, not if they can help us.'

Singh looked a little happier.

'I only know two of them,' he said. 'They were in my class at school. Mick Feaver and Jonty Marsh.'

'Feaver and Marsh,' Pascoe said. 'Do we know anything about them already?'

'Feaver's got no record,' Wield said. 'Marsh has been in trouble once or twice. You'll know his brother Arthur. Got a record as long as your arm. Stealing from houses, mainly.'

'OK,' Pascoe said. 'I'll speak to Marsh first. Bring him in.'

Wield watched quietly, admiring Pascoe's skill as he led the boy through his memories of what he had seen in the car park. Marsh remembered the BMW clearly, and its colour – dark blue.

'You're a good witness,' Pascoe said. 'Now, are you sure that the car the woman got out of was the car that got scratched?'

'Oh, yeah,' Marsh said. 'Dead certain.'

Pascoe said nothing, but let the boy realize for himself that his guilt was now clear.

Next, he talked to Mick Feaver. Mick remembered more details about the BMW. He also admitted that he had scratched Daphne's car.

Finally, Pascoe saw the two boys together.

'You have admitted damaging four cars,' he told them. 'This is serious, and we shall keep a record of it. However, you are both known to be of good character. One of my own officers tells me so. At the moment we shall go no further with this case. Please understand that you are very lucky, and keep out of trouble in future. Is that clear?'

'Yes, sir.' The boys were eager to escape.

When they had gone, Pascoe told Wield, 'You know, there's something very interesting about this dark blue BMW.'

'What's that, sir?'

'I know who it belongs to. I had to look at it recently because a garage door had fallen on it.'

'You mean it's Elgood's?'

'Yes. I've checked the description. It's definitely his.'

'Which means . . .'

'Which means – knowing Dick Elgood's reputation with women – we can be sure of one thing. The day before he came to tell us Patrick Aldermann was trying to murder him, he'd been off at his holiday cottage, making love to Aldermann's wife!'

CHAPTER 12

End of an affair

Dick Elgood was totally relaxed, floating on his back in the warm sea.

If he raised his head, he could look across the beach to his holiday cottage, which stood near the edge of a cliff.

Twenty years ago, when he had bought the cottage, it had not been so near the edge, but every winter the sea brought more of the cliff crashing down onto the beach.

Elgood did not worry about that. He had no child to leave the cottage to. He had bought it cheaply. He was rather fascinated by its impermanence and the way the coast was always changing.

Here he could relax, with a woman friend or alone. Today he wanted to be alone. He had had to deal with a difficult meeting the day before. Times were hard, and some of his workers were to lose their jobs, but he had managed the situation well, and now this sunny day of peace was his reward.

Or perhaps not. A car was stopping by the cottage. He thought for a moment of hiding, but knew he must face her. It was Daphne Aldermann. He swam to the beach.

'Hello, love,' he said. 'This is a nice surprise. How did you know I was here?'

'Patrick was talking to Eric Quayle on the phone last night. He told him.'

A car was stopping by the cottage. It was Daphne Aldermann.

Talking, were they, Elgood thought. Perhaps Patrick thought Quayle could get him onto the Board. Good thing he had made that phone call to London yesterday. That should put a stop to Aldermann's little plan.

He smiled at Daphne. 'Come up to the cottage, love, and have a cup of coffee. How long can you stay?'

As they climbed the cliff path, Daphne said, 'Doesn't it frighten you, the sea getting closer every year? It's pretty here, but it's so impermanent.'

'Not like Rosemont, you mean? But even Rosemont won't last for ever. Nothing will. I like change. It doesn't worry me.'

Daphne made the coffee while he got dressed. As soon as they sat down, she said, 'Dick, I came to tell you that it's over between us.'

He wasn't surprised. She had never been really interested in him, he could tell. This was no disappointment, and he found it easy to smile and say, 'Well, we're still friends. We've hurt no one. Don't feel guilty about it.'

His affair with Daphne had been unplanned and unexpected. He had met her when Aldermann joined the company as assistant to Chris Burke. He was charming to her, more from habit than because she attracted him, but he found her eager to meet him to discuss her husband's job and salary. He supposed that they were short of money. On several occasions he took her out for lunch.

Then Burke died, and Patrick took his job. Later, after Eagles had died, Elgood saw that Patrick hoped for a place on the Board, and knew that he didn't want him there. He was honest with Daphne, telling her how he felt. It was later the same day that he told Patrick, 'If you ever get a place on the Board, it'll be over my dead body!'

Dick Elgood did not expect to hear from Daphne again, but to his surprise she had telephoned, asking to see him. He had already planned a visit to his cottage next day, so he invited her to come with him. He was not sure she would come until the moment she had driven into the car park and jumped into his car.

All the way to the coast she talked nervously about Patrick. He still seemed to be so sure of success. It was as if he knew the future, knew for certain that he would be all right, and that he would always have Rosemont.

A few drinks at the cottage relaxed her, but she still looked worried and nervous when Elgood finally took her in his arms.

The next morning back at home the garage door had crashed down, narrowly missing him.

Now Daphne said, 'I'm really not the type to have an affair like this. I had to see you to make you understand. I felt so awful when the police came to ask questions about my car. I kept remembering those boys in the car park and wondering if they remembered me.'

The police were interested in your husband, not you, Elgood thought, but he could hardly tell her that!

'I must go in a minute. I feel better now we've talked,' Daphne said. 'I worry about such silly things. You know, recently I've met a woman and become friendly with her. She happens to be a policeman's wife. I like her a lot. She's really bright and independent. But I find myself waking up in the middle of the night thinking she's been told to spy on me!'

'Have you told Patrick about your new friend?' Elgood asked.

'Oh, yes. He wasn't bothered. He just told me to ask her and her husband to dinner.'

'What's her name?'

'Ellie Pascoe.'

To Daphne's horror, Elgood put his head in his hands and made a strange noise.

'Are you all right?' she asked in alarm.

'I wish I knew,' he said. 'Sit down again, Daphne. I've got something to tell you.'

CHAPTER 13

Past deaths and a future burglary

Dalziel laughed loudly when Pascoe told him over the phone about Elgood and Daphne Aldermann.

'It doesn't surprise me,' he said. 'It's just like Dick. Typical. Gives Aldermann a motive, though. And it explains why Dick seems so sure Aldermann's trying to kill him.'

'It surprised me,' Pascoe said. 'Ellie's got to know Daphne Aldermann quite well, and she doesn't seem the type.'

'Ask your Ellie what she can find out about the Aldermann woman,' Dalziel said.

'I don't think she'd like it if I asked her to spy on her friend, sir!'

'Why ever not?' Dalziel asked, sounding surprised. 'Here's some more information for you,' he went on. 'Another death close to Aldermann. Someone who wanted to buy Rosemont from Penny Highsmith about the time Patrick left school. Edgar Masson's the Aldermanns' family lawyer. He could tell you the details.'

'Anything else?'

'Yes. Ask him about Florence Aldermann's will. I'm so bloody bored with this conference, I've been out on the case instead. It seems Aunt Flo died without making a will. Another thing. Daphne's father had plenty of money to leave, but he didn't leave it all to her. If Aldermann expected to get rich that way, he was disappointed!

'I'd best be going now,' he went on. 'Somebody's giving a talk on the part policewomen can play in community relations.'

'And you don't want to miss it, sir?' said Pascoe, surprised.

'Don't be daft, lad. It'll be finishing soon, and the fool who's giving it has left his office open. I'm using his phone. He's locked his whisky away, though. Awful what suspicious minds some people have.'

'Why is Andy so interested in this case?' Pascoe said later to Wield. 'Before he went to London, he told us not to waste time on it. Now he's full of it. Why?'

'Because he's met Mrs Highsmith?' Wield suggested. 'Is he going to see her again soon?'

'I think he is,' Pascoe replied. 'Come on. Let's take a good look at what we already know.'

Wield listened, as Pascoe started to go through the list of events.

'1960. Mrs Florence Aldermann died of a heart attack. There are no suspicious circumstances, unless we count the fact that there was no will, so Penny Highsmith inherited everything. A few years later, Penny tried to sell Rosemont, but the buyer died. I'm seeing her lawyer, Masson, later today to talk about that.

'Now we jump forwards to 1971. The Reverend Oliver Somerton. Daphne Aldermann's father. He died in an accident at Little Leven church. There were no witnesses, which is always suspicious, but we know nothing else.

'On to 1976. Mrs Catherine McNeil. She died of flu, but we shouldn't be surprised by that. She was an old lady.'

'She's the one Aldermann had been robbing, isn't she?' Wield said. 'The one who left him her money?'

'That's her. It seems that Aldermann himself had flu, and while he was away from the office his boss found out about his little games with her money.'

'So Aldermann murdered her by sneezing over her and giving her flu,' Wield said. 'The sneeze as murder weapon. I must say it's an original sort of crime.'

'Let's leave the jokes to Mr Dalziel, shall we, Sergeant?' said Pascoe, and the two men laughed.

'1979,' Pascoe went on. 'Christopher Burke died, the first of three of Elgood's employees to meet a sudden death.'

'Fell off a ladder, didn't he?' Wield said.

'Yes. Some workmen were doing some repairs to his house. It seems he came home in the middle of the afternoon and ran up the ladder to see how the repairs were going. His foot slipped, and he fell and broke his neck.'

'Where were the workmen? Weren't there any witnesses?'

'No. It had been raining, so the workmen had gone off to do an indoor job somewhere else. Burke's wife had gone out. When she came home, she found her husband lying there dead.'

'Strange,' Wield said.

'What?'

'Running up a ladder in the middle of the afternoon, after it had been raining. Why wasn't he at his office? Do we know whether he had been drinking?'

'No,' Pascoe said, 'but if he was drunk, it might explain everything. We ought to look into it, Sergeant.

'Now,' he went on, 'we come to the final two deaths. Brian Bulmer, Elgood's financial director, crashed his car after the office party last Christmas. He was definitely drunk, I'm afraid. No one else was involved, and there were no witnesses.

Timothy Eagles, the chief accountant, had a heart attack, and died at his desk. He was found next morning, sitting there with his coat on. He must have been getting ready to go home, when he was taken ill.'

'Aldermann was his assistant, wasn't he?' said Wield. 'Shared an office with him?'

'Yes,' said Pascoe. 'What are you suggesting, Sergeant?'

Wield said, 'Imagine this. It's evening. Aldermann is about to leave the office. Everyone else has gone home. He finds Eagles at his desk, having his heart attack. He doesn't call for help. He just closes the door on him, goes home and leaves him to die.'

Pascoe let out a long whistle. 'Very cold-blooded. You've met Aldermann. Do you think he could do a thing like that?'

'It's easier than murder,' Wield said.

Pascoe sighed deeply. 'I don't know, Sergeant. Is this all what Dalziel would call "a load of daft rubbish", or is there really something going on? I just don't know.'

Police Cadet Shaheed Singh wondered what Mick Feaver wanted. When the boy had first come up to him, as he was going into the Market Café, he had expected anger. Now, seeing the expression on Mick's face and the cut on his lip, he felt sorry for him.

'Like a cup of tea?' Singh said. He would be meeting Wedderburn in the café in five minutes, so there was just time to hear what Mick wanted first. The boy followed him silently through the door. Mrs Pascoe was there, Singh noticed, but she was on her own this time.

'Look, Shady,' Mick said, as they sat down with their cups of tea, 'thanks for saying what you did yesterday.'

'Saying what I did?'

'Yeah. That Pascoe, he said someone had put in a good word for us. I knew it must be you.'

'That's all right.'

'Nothing's going to happen about scratching those cars, is it?'

'No.'

'We both admitted it,' Mick Feaver said. 'Pascoe knows it was all of us. That Jonty Marsh, he wanted to say it was just me, to let me be the only one to get into trouble. You should hear what he calls you, too. He says you pretend to be friendly, then go straight back to the Police Station and tell them everything you've heard.'

'Is that what he says?'

'That black pig, he calls you. That black pig.'

Singh looked down at his tea in silence. These had been his friends. What a distance there was between them now. Suddenly he wished he were in his father's shop, among the familiar sounds and smells of home.

'Look what they did to me last night,' Mick went on, touching his lip. 'They don't dare lay a finger on you, but they aren't afraid to have a go at me.'

Singh looked up. Mrs Pascoe was just going out of the door, he noticed, and Wedderburn was outside, talking to someone in the market.

'I've only got a moment,' he said. 'Is there something you want to tell me?'

Mick Feaver spoke in a sudden rush. 'It's Jonty Marsh. He's been boasting about his brother, Arthur. Says he's got a really big job on. Says Arthur's taking him along, too.'

Shaheed Singh found that he could not look up and meet the boy's eyes. So this was his first informer – his old schoolfriend Mick Feaver.

'The other lads didn't believe Jonty, see. Thought he was just talking big. So Jonty gets mad at them, says if they don't believe him, they can read all about it in the newspapers. It's going to be the first weekend in July. They're going to break into a big house called Rosemont.'

CHAPTER 14

Daphne gets angry

Ellie was not in a very good temper when the phone rang.

Before becoming Rose's mother, Ellie had been a teacher. She was continuing to do a little teaching even now, with a small baby to look after. This morning she was trying to mark a pile of tests she had given her students, and was finding it difficult to concentrate on them. She should have been marking them instead of waiting for Daphne in the café – and then Daphne had not even bothered to come!

She picked the phone up.

'I want to see you!' Daphne's voice said.

'Do you? You should have been at the Market Café, then, when I was sitting waiting for you!'

'I'm coming to see you now,' Daphne said, and put the phone down.

She sounded cold and unfriendly.

A short time later, she was at the door.

Ellie had decided to meet her with a smile.

'I'm glad to see you. You don't know how bored I was, marking these tests!'

'No, I don't know,' Daphne said. 'I'm too stupid to know anything, aren't I? I suppose you think I've got too much money and not enough sense, but at least I don't go around spying on my friends!'

She was pink with anger. It made her look very pretty, Ellie thought.

'Please sit down, Daphne,' she said, 'and tell me what this is all about.'

'Don't pretend you don't know. Just tell me one thing. Did you know from the start that *your* husband was investigating *mine*?'

'Oh dear,' Ellie said. 'This is difficult.'

'It's a simple question.'

'No, it isn't. Let's go back to the beginning. I gave you a lift in my car because it was raining. I didn't know who you were then. I kept on meeting you because I found I liked you.'

'To your great surprise!'

'Well, yes,' Ellie said. 'You are different from my other friends. I suppose I was quite pleased that I could get on so well with someone like you.'

'You're avoiding the main question,' Daphne said sourly, but she looked a little more relaxed.

'When you told me your name, and where your husband worked, I realized that Peter was investigating him, but I didn't do anything about it. I didn't want to ruin our friendship. Also, I like to keep some things in my life separate from my husband. In any case, the investigation didn't sound very serious.'

'If you wanted to be my friend, how could you discuss me with your husband?'

'I talked about you as a friend, that's all,' Ellie said. 'Please believe me. I'm sorry you're so upset about all this. What's happened to make you so angry all of a sudden?'

'Can't you guess? After all, you know everything about me. Dick Elgood told me.'

'About what?'

'About that stupid complaint he made to the police. He told me your husband was on the case. Then Dick told him to stop the investigation because it was all a silly mistake, but it's continuing, isn't it?'

'Yes,' Ellie said, 'I believe so. I don't know any details. You must believe me! But I don't understand. Why did Dick Elgood tell you this?'

'You really don't know?'

'No!'

'Then I'll tell you. When I parked my car, the day it was scratched, I was meeting Dick, to go to his cottage. I spent the day there with him.'

'Why, what did . . .' Ellie found herself unable to finish her question.

Daphne stared at her. 'I was having an affair with him. So you didn't know? How interesting that your husband hasn't told you. Or perhaps he doesn't know either. Will your deep friendship for me allow you to tell him, I wonder?'

She started to walk towards the door.

'Please stay, Daphne,' Ellie cried. 'We must talk some more.'

'Not now,' Daphne said coolly. 'Meet me tomorrow morning at the Chantry Coffee House. You can tell me then whether you've decided to tell your husband about me and Dick.'

CHAPTER 15

Pascoe goes visiting

Pascoe had quite a list of people to talk to. He wanted to see Masson, visit Capstick again, see Chris Burke's widow and talk to Elgood. And all for what? It could just be a waste of time.

First on the list was Masson, the Aldermanns' family lawyer.

The old man had reached the age when he was only too happy to talk to any visitor. All Pascoe had to do was listen, and every now and then guide the conversation back to the points he was interested in.

He learned that at the time of Florence Aldermann's death she had planned to change her will, and leave more money to her niece, Penelope Highsmith. Her original will left nearly everything to an animal charity and a church society, and only a very small amount of money to her niece. Then she had asked Penny to live at Rosemont and help look after the house, and, because of this, intended to increase her share of the money to forty per cent. However, she died before the new will could be made, and the old will was never found. Masson believed Mrs Aldermann had destroyed it herself, expecting to make a new one in a few days' time.

After Florence Aldermann's death, Masson had continued to act as lawyer for Penny. Pascoe asked him about the time when Penny had tried to sell Rosemont. A buyer had been found, but he had died before the sale could be completed.

'What did he die of?' Pascoe asked, hoping for a car accident in another country.

Masson's answer was worse than he would have believed possible.

'Poison,' said the old lawyer, enjoying the effect his answer caused.

It seemed that the man, who had been staying at a hotel, had eaten poisoned fruit. Perhaps he had picked an apple from a tree which had been treated with pesticide; perhaps it was the hotel's fault. Nobody knew. On the day he died he had been out in the country, but had stopped at Rosemont to discuss something about the sale with Penny Highsmith.

After that, Penny stopped trying to sell the house and moved to London. She divided the inheritance into two parts, kept the money, and gave Rosemont to Patrick, who was then a young man in his first job. Everyone expected him to sell the house, but instead he changed his name to Aldermann, and had been living at Rosemont ever since.

Here was plenty to think about, and Pascoe also had the feeling that, despite the old lawyer's willingness to talk, he had in fact said much less than he could have done. However, there were more calls to make. Second on his list was another visit to Little Leven, to talk to Mr Capstick.

Capstick was not at home, but his housekeeper was. Pascoe decided to ask her some questions instead.

'Can I ask you about the day the Reverend Somerton was killed? I know it was more than ten years ago, but perhaps you remember it.'

'Yes,' she said. 'I was here.'

'Mr Capstick was not at home that day, I understand.'

'No.'

'Was anyone else here?'

'Yes. The young man who used to look after the roses.'

Pascoe's heart raced with excitement.

'The roses? That was Mr . . .?'

'Aldermann, his name was. He took wonderful care of the roses. All I had to do was let him into the garden and leave him there.'

'Do you remember what time he left?'

'About four, I think.'

The Reverend Somerton's body had been discovered at four forty-five.

'Could I look at the garden?' Pascoe asked.

Among the flowers and overgrown bushes he found the little path, and the gate which opened into the church-yard. He stood silently among the graves. Death, he thought, was not the end of everything. The old must always give way to the new. Men died, and their bodies returned to the earth they came from, but new lives began, and year after year, century after century, the village lived on.

He knew all he needed to about Little Leven. It was time for his third visit.

He found Mrs Mandy Burke lying in a chair in her garden, enjoying the sun and a cool drink. She was wearing a bikini which left little to the imagination. Although well into her forties, she was still a good-looking woman, and one who clearly enjoyed life.

'Come and sit down,' she said, 'and let me pour you a drink.'

'Thank you, Mrs Burke,' said Pascoe. The iced fruit juice looked just what he needed on this hot afternoon, and he took a long swallow of it. It hit his throat like fire, making him spill some of it on his shirt as he coughed and gasped for breath. The 'juice' seemed to be at least half vodka.

'I'm so sorry,' Mandy Burke said. 'I should have warned you. Is it true you're not allowed to drink on duty? How very naughty of me to forget.'

'Never mind,' said Pascoe firmly, putting his glass down. 'Now I'm afraid I must ask you some questions about your husband's death, Mrs Burke.'

'Mandy,' she said. 'Do call me Mandy. Why do you want to ask me about poor old Chris after all this time? Don't think I'm hard-hearted, Inspector – or may I call you Peter? – but I've put all that behind me now. Life must go on, you know!'

She smiled at him over her glass.

'We're just making some routine enquiries,' Pascoe said. 'It won't take long. Would you mind telling me exactly what happened?'

'He climbed up a ladder,' she told him. 'We had some men here, doing some repairs to the house, but they weren't here that afternoon. I think Chris went up the ladder to check how much they'd done, his foot slipped and he fell. I was out at the time, and when I got home I found him just lying there, dead. He died instantly, Peter. At least that was some comfort to me.'

She wiped her eyes, and took a long drink.

'Isn't it hot?' she said. 'Do take your jacket off.'

'No. I must be going soon,' Pascoe said. 'Your husband was assistant to the chief accountant at Elgood Ceramics, wasn't he? Tell me, did you get to know any of his colleagues at all well?'

'I'm afraid I must ask you some questions about your husband's death, Mrs Burke,' said Pascoe.

'Well,' she said, 'we used to have dinner with Tim Eagles and his wife from time to time, and Mr Elgood was quite friendly. He was Chris's boss, of course. Chris didn't like Patrick Aldermann, the one who got his job. There'd been stories about him leaving a company after some sort of trouble. Chris never gossiped, but he didn't like what he heard about Mr Aldermann. He was a very straight man, was Chris, very honest.' She looked into her empty glass. 'Oh look, the drink's all gone. I'll just go into the kitchen and mix up some more.'

She stood up, nearly fell, and put one hand on Pascoe's shoulder to save herself.

Alarmed by this, he pulled back, and almost fell out of his chair.

'Careful!' she said. 'You haven't torn your trousers, have you? If you have, don't worry. I'm wonderful with a needle. I can sew them up so neatly, your wife will never notice they've been torn.'

'No, no, I'm fine,' Pascoe said. 'I really must be going now. Many thanks for all your help, Mrs Burke.'

He was glad to escape, but he had an uneasy feeling that, drunk and foolish as she was, Mandy Burke had told him only those things that she wanted him to know.

CHAPTER 16

More about Dick Elgood's love affairs

Pascoe wasn't sure what to think when Shaheed Singh came to him with his story about Mick Feaver and the planned burglary at Rosemont.

Dalziel, however, was full of enthusiasm when Pascoe told him about it over the phone.

'It's just the excuse you need to get back to Rosemont and have a good nose around,' he said. 'Tell them you need to check all the locks and windows. You never know what you might find out.'

Pascoe told him about his visits to Masson, Capstick, and Mandy Burke.

Dalziel asked several questions, then said, 'Does Masson think Penny destroyed her Aunt Flo's will?'

'I did wonder . . .' Pascoe said cautiously.

'I'm seeing her again on Friday night. I'll see what I can find out. And talking of wills, this Burke woman looked comfortable, did she?'

'Very,' said Pascoe. 'I think she's OK financially, too.'

'Don't be dirty, lad. You have a look into Mandy Burke's finances – see if there's anything that smells interesting.'

'I don't think he's been at that conference much,' Pascoe remarked to Wield. 'He seems to be much more interested in Mrs Highsmith at the moment.'

Pascoe's next job was to see Dick Elgood. It was immediately clear that Elgood was not pleased to see him.

'I told you to drop the case,' he said, 'but I hear you're still carrying on with your investigation.'

'I've got a job to do,' Pascoe said. 'Once we've started investigating a crime, we can't just stop suddenly.'

'Even if you have to ask your wife to spy on people?' said Elgood unpleasantly.

'You'd better explain that remark,' Pascoe said quietly.

'Was it just by chance that your wife first spoke to Mrs Aldermann the day after I came to see you?'

'I wonder how you know so much about Mrs Aldermann,' Pascoe said. 'Let me tell you what we know about her. We know that the day before you came to see me you spent the day with Mrs Aldermann at your holiday cottage.'

'I won't deny that. My private life is my own business.'

'You made it mine when you came to tell me her husband was trying to kill you,' Pascoe said.

'You mean Aldermann might be jealous? Rubbish! His roses are all he cares about. If I tried to take those away from him, he might get jealous!'

'Isn't that what you're trying to do by keeping him off your Board of Directors?'

'Maybe.' Elgood was suddenly serious. 'I'm doing what's best for the company. It will all be arranged at the Board meeting next week, when Aldermann is out of the way, visiting that fancy school he sends his boy to.'

'You'll wait until he's out of the way, yet you say you're not afraid of him?'

'No. I want you to forget all that. How many times do I have to tell you?'

Pascoe was about to leave, when the phone rang.

'It's for you,' Elgood said. 'Make it short. Some of us have got work to do.'

It was Sergeant Wield with some urgent information for Pascoe. Wield had been looking into Mandy Burke's finances. She ran her own small business, which was doing well. This was hardly surprising, as she had received a lot of help and advice from a well-known local businessman.

Pascoe put down the phone and turned to Elgood. 'I'm afraid I have one more question to ask you, Mr Elgood,' he said. 'What exactly is or was your relationship with Mrs Mandy Burke?'

To his surprise, Elgood gave in immediately.

'I may as well tell you,' he said, suddenly looking tired and old. 'You obviously know all about it. I've done nothing that's against the law. I'll tell you the truth. I was having an affair with Mandy Burke. She used to go to the cottage with me.'

He went on, 'We met in town by accident that day. We had lunch together, and then she suggested we went to her house. I thought it was too risky, but there was no stopping her! When I saw the workmen's ladder, I wanted to go immediately, but she said they'd finished for the day, and wouldn't be coming back.

'Well, to cut a long story short, we were in the bedroom when we heard a noise. Before I could stop her, Mandy ran to the window. She's like that, never thinks before she acts. She pulled back the curtains, and there was poor old Chris at the top of the ladder, like a monkey on a stick! I'll never forget his face. Mandy gave a great scream, and he fell. We rushed out, but he

73

was lying there, stone dead. We were shocked, Pascoe, believe me. Neither of us wanted to see poor old Chris Burke dead, but we had to protect ourselves. Didn't want the story all over the Sunday papers.'

'So you lied to the police.'

'He fell off a ladder. That was true.'

'I'll have to report this.'

'I won't repeat what I've just told you,' Elgood said. 'I'll deny everything. Mandy won't tell you anything, either. And, for God's sake, drop this Aldermann business, will you?'

While Peter Pascoe was talking to Dick Elgood, Ellie was sitting in the Chantry Coffee House with Rose, waiting for Daphne Aldermann. Daphne was late.

Ellie had decided to leave, when suddenly Daphne appeared at the door, rather pink in the face, as though she had been hurrying.

'I'm sorry I'm late,' she said. 'I forgot my purse, and had to go back home. When I got there, I found a man in the garden, who said he was from the water company. He said he'd come to deal with a problem with the pipes to our house. I don't know what he was talking about. I don't think there is a problem. Anyway, I got rid of him, and —'.

'Daphne,' Ellie interrupted, 'I shouldn't really tell you this, but Peter told me last night that there have been a lot of break-ins at big houses recently. He's been informed that Rosemont is on the thieves' list. It may not be true. He's going to come and see you about it.'

Daphne looked so alarmed that Ellie was almost sorry she had spoken.

Then Daphne said, 'I suppose you were discussing me and what I told you yesterday.'

'No. Honestly, I haven't told Peter anything,' Ellie said. 'He told me he was going to see Mr Elgood today, but I don't know why. Please believe me. We haven't been discussing you.'

'I believe you,' Daphne said. 'I must say I find it hard to imagine you as a police spy. Look, I've decided I want to tell you all about Dick and me, and about Patrick too.'

'Are you sure?'

'Yes. Not here, though. Let's go for a walk, if you don't mind.'

They left the Chantry Coffee House and walked around a quiet park in the sunshine as Daphne talked.

'I was worried about Patrick. It's difficult to explain why. He seems so sure all the time that he will get everything he wants. I don't know if he is hiding anything from me or not. Do you know why I started meeting Dick? Because I wanted to talk about Patrick, to find out how things were at work. Then, one lunch-time, Dick told me he didn't want Patrick on his Board of Directors.

'Then I began to worry about our financial position – the costs of our house and gardens are huge. I'd always left all that to Patrick. I knew I had some money from Daddy, and Patrick had some from his aunt, and from an old lady whose money he used to manage when he worked in Harrogate. We should have been able to manage all right, but suddenly I felt I had to know the details. So I challenged Patrick.

'Imagine how I felt, when he told me calmly that the money had all gone. We were in real financial difficulties, even though he had a good salary as chief accountant. Yet he told me everything would be all right. I screamed at him that he could forget his dream of being on the Board of Elgoods. He said it didn't matter. I said we would have to sell Rosemont. He told me that would never be necessary. I was afraid of him then. He seemed crazy.

'I rang Dick. I wanted to talk to him about Patrick. Dick asked me to go to the cottage with him. Of course I knew he took his women there, but I agreed. He listened to me. He was kind to me, charming in a rather old-fashioned way. Later, I realized I had frightened him. He thought I was warning him that Patrick got rid of people who were in his way, so he ran off to tell the police.'

'Yes,' Ellie said. 'He saw Peter.'

'Surely Peter doesn't think Patrick has done anything wrong? The way you describe Peter, he sounds such a sensible man.'

Ellie did not answer Daphne's question.

'You'll have a chance to meet Peter soon,' she said. 'He wants to see you and Patrick before you both go away next week.'

'Fine,' Daphne said. 'He can come and see us on Saturday.'

The two women left the park in a state of friendship which they both knew might turn out to be the calm before the storm.

CHAPTER 17

Dalziel has a wonderful time

Penny Highsmith enjoyed her food and drink, but she could not compete with Andy Dalziel, with whom she was having dinner at a restaurant. The amount of good red meat and good red wine he was working his way through had the waiters staring in disbelief.

He was also enjoying being in the company of an attractive and intelligent woman, and he told Penny so.

'I'm so glad, Andy,' she said. 'I had been wondering if you found me again just by chance, or whether there was some deliberate plan behind it.'

'You mean we were supposed to meet? Written in the stars? That sort of thing?'

'Not exactly. Police investigations is more what I was thinking. But now I see you enjoying yourself so much, I don't believe you can be pretending.'

'Of course not. I'm having a wonderful time.'

'Good. Of course, I did check on you with Patrick, when I saw him yesterday.'

'Oh,' Dalziel said, surprised. 'Did he stay long?'

'No. He never does. We've never been terribly close.'

'Strange, after you brought him up by yourself. Did you never think of marrying his dad?'

'Mind your own business.'

'Sorry. But it must have been hard.'

'Some people were less than kind to me, but it wasn't so bad. Aunt Flo and Uncle Eddie were very generous.'

'And then she left you Rosemont and all that money. Were you surprised when you heard the will?'

He watched her carefully. He had been thinking about Pascoe's discussion with Masson, and he had some ideas of his own.

'There was no will,' Penny said. 'I inherited because I was her only living relation.'

'And Patrick, of course.'

'Oh yes. Patrick always loved Rosemont. Aunt Flo was the ambitious one. She wanted the big house. Eddie wasn't interested in that, but he loved the gardens, especially the roses.'

'Just like Patrick.'

'Oh yes. I prefer London. There's more life here. I'm a city girl, myself.'

'Patrick must have been upset when your uncle died.'

'He was,' she said, 'although he never shows things like that. I think he loved Eddie more than he loved me. I tried to tell him that we might not be going to Rosemont again, after Eddie died, but it was strange, he took no notice of me. He was sure he would be staying at Rosemont for ever. And of course he was right. But why are we talking about all this?'

'Just passing the time. So Aunt Flo dropped dead in the rose garden, and fortunately for you she had just torn up her will.'

Immediately her face changed. Her black curls shook with anger.

'What are you saying? That I destroyed the will? Is that it?'

Her voice had risen almost to a shout and people were

looking at them, but it was impossible to embarrass Dalziel.

'Well, didn't you? No one would blame you if you did.'

Penny sprang to her feet, almost knocking over her chair.

'You fat pig!' she shouted. 'You don't change! I'm not staying here with you another moment!'

He watched her disappear through the door. Then he paid the bill, and picked up her bag, which she had left on a chair.

In the street, he called a taxi and got into it, leaving the door open. In a second Penny appeared, and got into the taxi too.

'Can I have my bag?' was all she said.

At the door to her flat she tried to go in alone, but Dalziel put his shoulder in the door.

'Listen,' he said. 'I've really enjoyed this evening. It's been grand. Thank you.'

She gave him a puzzled look.

'What are you really after?'

'Friendship. That's all. Look, just let me come in and check your flat for burglars. London is a dangerous place for a woman to live on her own.'

She laughed, so he went ahead.

'Seems OK,' he said. 'I'll just check the bedroom.'

With the confidence of someone who is not expecting trouble, he opened the door. The man standing behind the door hit him hard on the nose, then rushed past to the front door, knocking Penny to the floor as he went.

Dalziel's eyes filled with water. As he rubbed them, he saw Penny struggling to get up. Her lovely black hair seemed to have moved somehow, and underneath it other hair, short and grey, could be seen.

'Are you all right?' he asked.

Dalziel took off his tie and sat down.

'Yes, even though you're still here! What should I do, call the police?'

'I am the police, remember?' Dalziel said. He helped her up and they went round the flat. The burglar had been neat, and did not seem to have taken anything. Dalziel advised her to change her door locks. Then he took off his tie and sat down.

'What do you think you're doing?' Penny protested.

'I can't leave you all alone after a shock like that,' he said, 'now can I? You need a friend with you at a time like this.'

For a moment she looked angry. Then she smiled, took off the black wig, and ran her fingers through her short grey hair. Suddenly, she looked fifteen years older.

'I can take my teeth out, too,' she said.

'Grand, love,' Dalziel said. 'I was afraid I might be too old for you.'

CHAPTER 18

Everything is explained – or is it?

Daphne Aldermann got up on Saturday morning with a feeling that an important decision would be made that day.

Since talking with Ellie Pascoe, she had spent a lot of time thinking about her marriage. She had decided that it was time to be open and honest with Patrick if they were to have a future together. She was waiting for him to come home from his two days in London. He had rung to say that he would be home mid-morning.

As Patrick came through the door, however, she realized immediately that this was not the right time for a serious discussion. He was smiling, looking happier and more relaxed than he had for a long time, and carrying a beautiful bunch of roses.

They were golden roses, edged with pink, and they had a sweet, delicate perfume.

'Darling, they're beautiful. But I can't imagine you *buying* roses!' Daphne said. 'What are they?'

'Look at the label.'

The name on the label was 'Daphne Aldermann'. Daphne stared at it, puzzled.

'Don't you remember?' Patrick said. 'Years ago, I said one day I'd create a lovely new rose, and I'd give it your name. It's taken me six years, but now here it is!' He was laughing with excitement and happiness.

'It's wonderful!' Daphne said. 'Patrick, I'm so . . .'

'That's not all,' he went on. 'This rose is going to be grown commercially. It will be on sale everywhere. And I've written a book all about it, which will be sold at the same time. It's what I've always wanted.'

'And you kept all this a secret. It's quite a shock to find out about it now,' Daphne said slowly.

'I didn't want to say anything until I knew it would all be a success.'

Everything was clear now, Daphne thought. His strange, secretive behaviour, the way he seemed so sure of the future. She hadn't understood what was happening. She'd gone to Dick Elgood. He'd gone to the police. It was all her fault, all of it.

'There's money in this rose and in the book,' Patrick said. 'It means I can tell Dick Elgood I don't want to be on his Board of Directors. Oh, I know he doesn't want me, anyway. I'll stay in my present job and have more time for my roses and my book.'

'Oh Patrick, I'm so glad!' Daphne said. She wondered how she could have been so foolish. This would be a fresh start for them both.

They were in the middle of a long and passionate kiss when the door bell rang. In alarm, Daphne remembered that the police were calling to discuss the possible burglary. She hurriedly explained all this to Patrick, and then went to open the door.

When Peter Pascoe and Sergeant Wield came into the room, Pascoe was surprised by the warm and friendly atmosphere. It was the first time he had seen Daphne. He found her beautiful, and, as Ellie had said, very attractive. Both she and Patrick seemed so relaxed and happy, he guessed that something unusual had just happened.

'We've checked with the water company,' Pascoe told them. 'They haven't sent anyone to your house, so I'm afraid we are expecting an attempted break-in. I need to look at your security arrangements and check every room in the house.'

Daphne took him around the house, while Patrick talked to Sergeant Wield in the living-room. When they were upstairs, Daphne told Pascoe everything, about Patrick's success with the new rose, her mistaken ideas about him, and her affair with Elgood.

'But now everything will be all right,' she finished. 'Patrick is going to tell Dick Elgood he isn't interested in his Board of Directors.'

'I see,' Pascoe said. 'Well, it never seemed much of a motive for murder. And Mr Aldermann has never seemed a particularly ambitious man.'

'Or the type to murder people, I hope!' Daphne said.

Pascoe smiled. He did not want to tell her that the most charming people are sometimes killers.

'I'm pleased for you,' he said. 'Ellie will be pleased, too.'

His pleasure at Aldermann's success was real. His investigations had shown him that the man had bad financial problems. Now they would be over. He liked Daphne, and was happy to think that Ellie had chosen her as a friend.

As he and Wield moved towards the front door, the phone rang and Daphne went to answer it. 'It's for you, darling,' she called to Patrick. 'It's Dick Elgood.' Patrick went over to the phone.

At the front door, Daphne gave Pascoe her hand.

'I hope we'll see more of you and Ellie,' she said.

'I'd like that,' Pascoe replied.

Back at the Police Station, Dalziel was also in a good mood. First, he had congratulated Shaheed Singh on his good work with Mick Feaver. Second, he had had a most interesting talk with Penny Highsmith's lawyer, Edgar Masson. After hearing Pascoe's report on Masson, Dalziel had asked the old lawyer to come and see him. They had known each other for a long time, and Dalziel had decided to try the 'old friends' approach on him.

'You must have suspected that Mrs Highsmith had destroyed Florence Aldermann's will,' he told Masson. 'Why did you do nothing about it?' He refilled Masson's whisky glass.

'Because that way justice would be done,' the old lawyer said. 'I see that I must explain something to you, Mr Dalziel, but it must not go beyond these four walls. I was absolutely certain that, when Eddie Aldermann died three years previously, Florence had deliberately destroyed his will.'

'Why would she do that? Surely he had left her most of his money? I mean, she *was* his wife.'

'He was the kindest and fairest of men. Of course he left most of his property to his wife. But he also left a large amount to Penelope Highsmith, for her son Patrick to have when he was older. Do you understand what I'm trying to tell you, Mr Dalziel?'

'Say it. Straight out with it.'

'Eddie Aldermann was Patrick's father.'

CHAPTER 19

Dick Elgood gives a party

That Saturday had begun well for Dick Elgood. At eleven o'clock he was sitting in his office, waiting for a visitor.

The visitor wore dark glasses and a hat, so that he would be difficult to recognize. Daphne had seen him, and he had pretended to be from the water company. Dalziel had surprised him at Penny Highsmith's flat. He was Raymond Easey, a private detective.

Easey's job had been to gather evidence of Patrick Aldermann's financial difficulties. He had done that well, and he had done more than that. He had followed Aldermann to a London flat, discovered that it belonged to his mother, and waited until he had seen her go out with a fat man. Then he had searched the flat and found an interesting document – Florence Aldermann's will.

Dick Elgood was clearly delighted to see the will.

'Do you think she'll realize it's gone?' he asked.

'I don't think so. People put something in a safe place, and then forget where it is.'

Easey was right. The will really had been lost after Aunt Florence's death. Then Penny had found it, and put it away while she decided what to do. Her lawyer, Masson, had suggested that the lack of a will meant that she would get the money Eddie had wanted her to have. She thought about it. The will remained hidden. Finally, she forgot all about it.

Elgood paid Easey a large amount of money, and when the detective had left, he telephoned Patrick Aldermann.

'Listen to me,' he said. 'I've got a document here that would interest you. It's a will. It seems that that great big house and garden of yours have never really belonged to you at all.'

There was a long pause. Then Patrick said calmly, 'I'd be interested to see this document. Are you at your office? Can I come and see it now?'

Easey had gone, and Elgood was alone in the building.

'No,' he said. 'Don't do that. I'm leaving the office now, but I'll be at the cottage tomorrow. I'm having a lunch party. Why don't you come? Bring the family. Oh, and bring a letter, too, saying you withdraw from your attempt to get a place on the Board.'

'Certainly,' Patrick said politely. 'Where exactly is the cottage?'

'Ask Daphne,' Elgood said. 'She'll know where it is.'

Afterwards, he thought that that had been an unnecessary, and possibly unwise, remark to make. Then he put it out of his mind. He made a copy of the will, and locked the original in a drawer in his desk. Then he started phoning people to invite them to lunch. Among his guests were his old friend Andy Dalziel and Dalziel's young Inspector, Peter Pascoe.

The following day was hot, and the guests at the party spent much of their time lying on the beach in the sun or swimming. Most of the children had taken off their clothes, and the women wore only the briefest of bikinis. Even Dalziel had taken off his jacket.

'Look at Andy!' Ellie whispered to Pascoe. 'That nose looks terrible. Do you really believe that story about a burglar in Patrick's mother's flat? I think it was really Penny herself who hit him!'

'I don't think so,' Pascoe said. 'From what I've heard, I think she and Andy rather enjoyed meeting each other again.'

Daphne came out of the sea and threw herself down on the beach next to Ellie. 'Isn't this lovely?' she said.

'Yes,' said Ellie. 'You look very happy today, Daphne. I'm so glad everything seems to be going well for you and Patrick.'

'Yes. It's like a story with a happy ending for us!'

Elgood was an attentive host, moving among his guests with a word and a smile for everyone, but he did not stop until he reached Patrick Aldermann.

'Patrick, come up to the cottage with me,' he said. 'I've been trying to make a little garden here, but I can't get anything to grow. If anyone can advise me, you can.'

'Of course,' Patrick said. 'It will be a pleasure.'

The two men went together across the beach and up the cliff path. Dalziel watched them go.

'True friendship,' he said in Pascoe's ear. 'Does you good to see it. What's that rubbish you're drinking?'

'Actually, sir, it's a very pleasant wine I'm taking to Ellie,' Pascoe said.

'That's another thing. When I was married, I'd never have let my wife lie around on a beach in one of those bikini things.'

He gave a loud and unpleasant laugh.

'Well, it's too hot for me here. I'm going to find somewhere cool, inside. Sun boils your brains, you know. That's why most foreigners are half daft.'

Pascoe sighed. It was clear that too much whisky, as well as too much sun, was affecting Dalziel. He took Ellie her drink, and then followed his boss up the cliff path.

Patrick Aldermann was standing alone in the doorway of the cottage.

'Where's Dick?' asked Dalziel.

'Having a shower,' Patrick told him.

'Why does he want a shower? He's just been in the sea, hasn't he?' said Dalziel, and he pushed past Patrick and went into the kitchen to see what he could find in Elgood's fridge.

Pascoe caught Aldermann's eye, and the two men smiled.

'Let me give you these now,' Aldermann said, handing Pascoe a bunch of keys. They had arranged, during Pascoe's visit to Rosemont, that while Patrick and Daphne were away, the police would wait in the house at night, hoping to catch the burglars red-handed.

'Thank you,' Pascoe said. 'We'll take great care of your house, sir. And the garden, of course. You're leaving in the morning, I believe?'

'Yes. Look, please don't call me "sir". Our wives have become so friendly with one another. Call me Patrick.'

Pascoe smiled. 'Thank you, Patrick. And you must call me Peter.'

At that moment Elgood came into the hall, and took Patrick out into the garden.

'One of your problems here is salt, of course,' Patrick told him, 'and another is insects. You need to do something about them, or they'll eat everything you plant.'

'Oh, I've got some stuff for them,' Elgood said. He took Patrick back into the cottage and showed him a large box full of bottles.

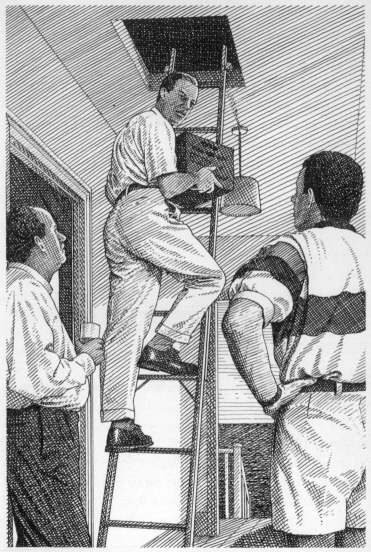

Elgood carried the box up the ladder. 'Satisfied now?' he said to Patrick.

Patrick bent over to look. 'You've got enough chemicals here to kill all the insects in Yorkshire!' he said disapprovingly. 'This is dangerous stuff. You shouldn't leave it where children could find it.'

'All right, all right,' Elgood said, rather annoyed. 'I'll put it somewhere safe.'

He reached up and opened a small door in the ceiling. A folding ladder came down.

'There's some space up there by the water tank,' he said. 'I had to get a new tank when I had the shower put in.'

He carried the box up the ladder.

'Satisfied now?' he said to Patrick.

'Nice place you've got here, Dick,' Dalziel said, coming out of the kitchen with a glass in his hand. 'Just the right size for a loving couple.'

'Remind me to invite you some time, Andy,' Elgood replied.

The rolls of fat on Dalziel's stomach shook with laughter. 'That would really give people something to gossip about!' he said. 'You staying here tonight, Dick?'

'No. I've got to be in the office early tomorrow. I'll be here again on Tuesday night. I like to have a swim and relax here before a really important meeting.'

He gave Patrick a pitying look, which Pascoe thought was rather unpleasant of him.

Meanwhile, on the beach, Daphne was saying to Ellie, 'I think for the first time I really understand Patrick. Everything is so wonderful at the moment. I can't tell you how happy we are.'

CHAPTER 20

Shaheed Singh sees some action

Wield and Singh sat in silence in one of the bedrooms at Rosemont. The night air was perfumed by the hundreds of roses below them in the gardens.

Pascoe and another man were also in the house, while two others were outside in a car.

Singh was nervous, wide-awake and eager for his first taste of action. Wield was bored. Slowly, the hours passed.

When it was light, Pascoe came into the room. He gave a yawn.

'All right. That's enough. Go down to the kitchen and get some coffee. We'll try again tonight.'

They went downstairs. As he passed Patrick Aldermann's study, Pascoe heard a noise. He opened the door, and found Dalziel looking through some papers in the desk.

'Come in, Peter. Had a good night, have you?' Dalziel asked.

'What are you doing here?' Pascoe demanded. 'Sir?'

'I thought you might need some company. Nothing's happened, has it? I didn't think it would, but I didn't want to stop you when you were enjoying yourself so much. Let's take a walk round the garden.' Dalziel sounded friendly and relaxed.

What the hell did he want? Pascoe wondered.

As they walked around the rose garden, he asked Dalziel, 'Do you still suspect Patrick Aldermann of something, sir?'

'Me? No. Why should I? A lot of people have died, it's true, but people are always dying, aren't they? And we've no bodies, have we? That's what we're short of, Peter. Bodies.'

He sounded almost regretful, Pascoe thought. They went back into the house, and had breakfast with Wield and Singh.

'Are we leaving now?' Pascoe asked, when everyone had finished.

'Oh no,' Dalziel said. 'We're here to catch some burglars, aren't we? We're staying.'

He led them back upstairs, and then lay down on a bed.

'Wake me up when they come,' he said, and appeared to fall asleep.

Just after eight o'clock they heard a noise, and saw an old van coming into the garden. They could see *Caldicott and Son, Gardeners* written on it.

'They're here,' Dalziel said, sitting up.

'The gardeners!' Pascoe exclaimed. 'Is it them?'

'There's Jonty Marsh,' Singh said. 'I can see him! And Arthur!'

'Clever, isn't it?' Dalziel said. 'People need their gardeners to call, even when they are away on holiday. And the gardeners have plenty of time to study the house and decide what they want to steal.'

'They aren't stealing anything, sir,' Wield said. 'So far, they're just doing their job.'

'Give them time,' Dalziel told him. 'One of them will cut the burglar alarm. One will come into the house. The others will stay in the garden, so everything looks nice and normal.'

He's right! Pascoe thought bitterly. He saw all this and I didn't. He may be old and fat, I may make jokes about him and laugh at him behind his back, but he's still a better policeman than I am.

Ten minutes went by before they heard someone come into the house.

'Let's go,' Dalziel said. 'You stay here, Singh. We don't want any cadets to get hurt.'

They ran downstairs and found Arthur Marsh in the study with a bag in his hand. As Marsh turned to run, Dalziel threw his considerable weight forwards and held onto his leg.

But Arthur was not the only burglar in the house. Jonty Marsh, with a heavy silver candle-stick in his hand, pushed past Wield and ran upstairs into one of the bedrooms. Wield followed him.

There was shouting, a cry, a crash and then silence.

Wield ran into the room, to find Singh lying on the floor, blood pouring from his head. Through the window, he caught sight of the old van, blocked now by a police car.

Then there was another cry, and he saw Jonty Marsh hanging white-faced outside the window. Wield put all his strength into pulling the criminal in, although he would rather have tried to help the young police cadet lying unconscious at his feet. It was impossible to say whether he was alive or dead.

CHAPTER 21

'Nothing ever really changes'

On Tuesday night Dick Elgood arrived at the cottage too late to have a swim. Unusually for him, the whispering of the sea in the dark night made him feel lonely and low-spirited, but he woke up next day to a sunny morning, and his mood became more cheerful.

After breakfast he swam, coming out of the sea refreshed in mind and body, ready for the day ahead. He walked back to the cottage and went straight to the shower. The warm water washed the salt off him, and he had enjoyed the sensation for several minutes before he noticed that anything was wrong. His skin began to feel sore and painful. At first it wasn't too bad. His eyes felt as if they had soap in them. He opened them to wash it out.

He screamed as the full force of the pain hit him. His eyes seemed to be on fire, and he crashed about blindly as he tried to run from the cottage and find his way down to the sea. Only the sea, he felt, could make him clean, could save him from this pain. At last he fell into the waves, and the sea washed over his body.

Pascoe, Dalziel, and Wield had just been to visit Shaheed Singh. The young man lay in a hospital bed, his head heavily bandaged, but with a smile on his face. He was not seriously hurt, and the praise and kind words from those he thought of as his bosses were already making him feel better. Soon his parents and his brothers and sisters would be coming to see him, all proud of the policeman in their family. He had helped to catch a gang of thieves, and was happier than he had been for a long time.

Back at the station, it was Dalziel who heard the news first. He rushed into Pascoe's office, shouting, 'He's dead! Dick Elgood's dead!'

'How?'

'Drowned. His body's been found in the sea near his cottage.'

'What happened? A heart attack?'

'We don't yet know. Find out, can you?'

Hours later, Pascoe had his answer. He looked shocked as he told Dalziel, 'All those bottles of pesticide and stuff he had to kill the insects in his garden. When he put them up in his roof, they must have fallen into his water tank, so that the poisons came out of his shower. Poor Elgood. He died a horrible death. It must have been an accident.'

'Do you really believe that, Inspector?' Dalziel asked in a hard voice.

'It must have been. You surely don't think Patrick Aldermann is involved? Where's the motive? The business about the Board is all over. And the opportunity? He's been away since Monday, and on Sunday night he and Daphne were at our house.'

'Were they indeed,' Dalziel said. 'And later? He could have left his family asleep and driven back to the coast.'

'I suppose so. I'm sure Daphne would know if he went out again that night.'

'Ask her,' Dalziel said. 'You're going there to talk to them about the burglars, aren't you? Ask her then.'

Pascoe hesitated, and then said, 'If I must, sir.'

'Oh yes,' Dalziel told him. 'You know you bloody well must.'

Pascoe arrived at Rosemont in the middle of a golden afternoon. Daphne opened the door to him.

'Peter!' she cried, 'how nice to see you! Come in. Ellie's here. We're all out in the garden.'

'Have you heard about Dick Elgood?'

Her face changed. 'Yes. It's terrible news. Was it a heart attack while he was swimming?'

He was sure she wasn't acting.

He went into the garden and found Ellie there, with Rose and the two Aldermann children. David, the Aldermanns' son, had been upset by the news of the burglary, and Patrick and Daphne had brought him home from school with them.

'I'm here on business,' Pascoe told Ellie quietly.

Daphne brought out drinks for the children.

'Poor Dick,' she said to Ellie. 'You know, it's funny, but I felt on Sunday that I might be seeing him for the last time.'

'Really?' Ellie clearly found this hard to believe.

'Yes, really. I couldn't sleep. I sat out here in the garden, feeling something terrible was about to happen.'

'What about Patrick?' Pascoe asked. 'Did he feel the same?'

'Oh no!' Daphne laughed. 'He slept as well as he always does.'

Pascoe felt a great relief. Clearly, Patrick had been safely at home all that night.

'Where is Patrick?' he asked. 'I think I'll go and have a word with him.'

'In his rose garden, of course,' Daphne said. 'He's upset over Dick's death. He always turns to his roses when he feels sad.'

Pascoe found Patrick deadheading the roses with his sharp knife.

'There's so much to do,' he said, continuing to work as they talked.

'And now you've lost your gardeners.'

'Yes. It's a great disappointment. Old Caldicott's father worked for Uncle Eddie, you know. How could they do such a thing?'

'It was Brent, the son,' Pascoe told him. 'He met Arthur Marsh in prison. Old Caldicott really didn't want to be involved. He told us he admired you, and thought you were a *real* gardener, unlike most people. But he was short of money, and I'm afraid Brent must have persuaded him to join in the burglary.'

'It was a shock,' Aldermann said, 'but Dick Elgood's death is a worse one. Such a terrible waste. But then so much of his life was a waste.'

'He looked successful enough to me,' Pascoe said.

'Did he? I suppose he thought he was a success, but I don't think he was a truly happy man.'

'What will happen to Elgood Ceramics now?'

'I don't know. There will be changes. But nothing ever really changes.'

Patrick spoke with the calm of one who knows the truth about life. Everything had always happened as he knew it would. Today he had gone to Elgood's office. In the confusion it had been easy to find the original of Aunt Florence's will in the desk drawer, and to remove it. He had not felt that he was

*The sun shone suddenly on the knife, as it moved among
the dead and dying flowers.*

taking a risk. In the same way, it had been easy to wander into the cottage while Elgood's guests were saying goodbye, to pull down the folding ladder, and to put the box of garden chemicals into the water tank, with the bottle tops loosened. Three minutes. Nobody had seen him. This was right. This was how it was meant to be, how it had been and how it always would be.

David came running out to his father.

'Mummy says bring Mr Pascoe into the house for a drink now,' he said.

Of course,' Patrick said, continuing to cut off the deadheads. 'I'm sorry, Peter. I'm not being a very good host, am I?'

The sun shone suddenly on the knife, as it moved among the dead and dying flowers.

'Daddy,' said the little boy.

'Yes, David?'

'Why are you doing that? What's it for?'

'Well . . .' Aldermann paused and then smiled, as if at a private joke.

He closed the knife, and put it in his pocket.

'I'll tell you some other time. We have our guests to look after. Come on, Peter, you must be hot. Let's join Daphne and Ellie for a cool drink. Isn't it a perfect day?'

Exercises

A   Checking your understanding

Chapters 1–5 *How much can you remember? Check your answers.*
1 How old was Patrick at the time of Florence Aldermann's death?
2 What kind of business did Richard Elgood run?
3 Why couldn't Daphne use her own car to take her daughter to school?
4 How did Daphne and Ellie meet for the first time?
5 What was Patrick Aldermann's chief interest in life?
6 What did Patrick give to Pascoe the first time they met?

Chapters 6–11 *Find answers to these questions in the text.*
1 What was the reason Pascoe gave Dalziel for wanting to investigate Patrick Aldermann?
2 How did Daphne's father die?
3 Who gave Shaheed Singh some important information about Daphne?
4 Why did Patrick lose the first job he ever had?
5 Why hadn't Penny Highsmith been able to sell Rosemont?
6 What did Pascoe discover about Elgood and Daphne?

Chapters 12–16 *Are these sentences true (T) or false (F)?*
1 Dick Elgood and Daphne were very much in love.
2 Shaheed Singh discovered a plan to break into Rosemont.
3 Ellie knew all about Daphne's affair with Elgood before Daphne told her.
4 Patrick had the opportunity to kill the Reverend Somerton.
5 Mandy Burke was eager to give the police any help she could.
6 Elgood and Mandy Burke wanted to kill Chris Burke.

Exercises

Chapters 17–21 *What is your opinion about these questions?*

1 What do we learn about Penny Highsmith's character from her evening with Dalziel?
2 Daphne feels very guilty when Patrick tells her about his new rose and his book. Is she right to feel like that?
3 What does the attempted burglary at Rosemont tell us about Dalziel?
4 How would you describe Patrick's position at the end of the book?

B Working with language

1 *Complete these sentences with information from the story.*

1 Elgood went to the police because . . .
2 It is possible that Patrick killed Eagles by . . .
3 Capstick still missed Patrick, although . . .
4 Daphne was angry with Ellie when . . .
5 Penny Highsmith inherited Rosemont because . . .
6 Jonty Marsh injured Shaheed Singh by . . .

2 *Combine these sentences into longer sentences, using linking words and making any other necessary changes. Write them as a paragraph.*

Patrick Aldermann and his family were away from home.
Six policemen spent the night at Rosemont.
They were hoping to catch a gang of burglars.
Nothing happened that night.
In the morning, Pascoe found Dalziel in the house.
He was looking through Patrick's papers.
Pascoe asked him if they were leaving.
Dalziel told him to wait.
They would catch the burglars first.
The gardeners arrived in their van.
Pascoe realized that they were the burglars.
The police caught them.
Shaheed Singh was injured in the struggle.
He was not seriously hurt.
He was hit over the head with a heavy candle-stick.

104

C Activities

1 Write a short description of your favourite female character in this story.
2 Do you think Shaheed Singh will go on to become a successful policeman? Write a paragraph about the particular problems he faces.
3 Write a short essay comparing the characters of Pascoe and Dalziel and describing their relationship.
4 'We must find the courage to reach out and take what life offers us.' Do you agree with Patrick Aldermann?
5 How many deaths do you think Patrick was responsible for? Were any of them actually murder? The detective's classic question about a suspected murderer is: did he have motive, means, and opportunity? Write a report describing the deaths of the eight people below, and making a case either for or against Patrick.
   Mrs Florence Aldermann
   The man who was going to buy Rosemont House from Penny
   The Reverend Somerton
   Mrs McNeil
   Chris Burke
   Brian Bulmer
   Timothy Eagles
   Dick Elgood

Glossary

accountant a person whose job is to keep and examine records of money received or paid out by a business

accounts record books which show money received or paid out by a business or an individual

affair a sexual relationship, usually secret, between two people who are not married to one another

Asian (*n* or *adj*) a person from one of the countries in Asia (e.g. India or Pakistan)

bikini a woman's two-piece swim-suit

blonde (*adj*) golden or yellow-haired

bloody (*adj*) a swearword used to emphasize an angry statement or an order

blue moon from the expression 'once in a blue moon', meaning very rarely or never

bush a large flowering plant, for example, a rosebush

cadet a young person who is training to become a police officer

ceramics objects made of porcelain or china, such as sinks and toilets

chairman the chief official in a company or other organization

charity an organization which exists to help people in need

conference a meeting, especially a large one, for discussion or exchange of opinions

daft (*adj, informal*) silly, foolish

darling a name you call someone you like or love

dead (*adv, informal*) completely, absolutely

elegant tasteful and stylish in appearance or manner

flu (*informal*) short for influenza, an illness like a bad cold with muscle pain and fever

greenhouse a building with glass walls and roof, used for growing plants that need a warm place

lad (*informal*) a boy or young man

middle-class (*adj*) the class of society between the lower and upper, which includes business and professional people

multi-storey (*adj*) a tall building with many floors

nose around (**have a nose around**) to look with curiosity, to see what you can find

passionate (*adj*) full of emotion, especially love

pesticide a poison used by farmers or gardeners to kill insects

petal one of the delicate, coloured, leaf-like parts of a flower

Reverend used as the title of a clergyman

sergeant a police officer below the level of an inspector

sexy sexually attractive

stress unhappiness or illness caused by overwork or difficult circumstances

stuff (*n*) a slang word for any unnamed things, belongings, etc.

superintendent a police officer above the level of a chief inspector

tank a container for liquid, for example, petrol or water

tasty (*slang*) attractive, good-looking

treat (*n*) something that gives pleasure, especially when it is a surprise

van a covered vehicle, with no side windows, for carrying goods or people

vandal a criminal who damages public or private property just for fun

wander to walk around slowly and aimlessly

wig a covering for the head made of real or artificial hair

will (*n*) a legal document which states who should inherit your money or property after you die

youth (*n*) a young man, especially a teenager (usually an uncomplimentary word)